*Routledge Revivals*

# THE PSYCHOLOGY OF THE CRIMINAL

# THE PSYCHOLOGY OF THE CRIMINAL

BY

# M. HAMBLIN SMITH, M.A., M D.

LATE MEDICAL OFFICER OF H.M. PRISON, BIRMINGHAM ; LATE
LECTURER ON CRIMINOLOGY IN THE UNIVERSITY OF BIRMINGHAM ;
LECTURER IN CRIMINOLOGY AT BETHLEM ROYAL HOSPITAL, LONDON

First published in 1933 by Methuen & Co. Ltd.

This edition first published in 2018 by Routledge
2 Park Square, Milton Park, Abingdon, Oxon, OX14 4RN
and by Routledge
711 Third Avenue, New York, NY 10017

*Routledge is an imprint of the Taylor & Francis Group, an informa business*

© 1933 Taylor & Francis

All rights reserved. No part of this book may be reprinted or
reproduced or utilised in any form or by any electronic, mechanical,
or other means, now known or hereafter invented, including photocopying
and recording, or in any information storage or retrieval system, without
permission in writing from the publishers.

**Publisher's Note**
The publisher has gone to great lengths to ensure the quality of this reprint
but points out that some imperfections in the original copies may be
apparent.

**Disclaimer**
The publisher has made every effort to trace copyright holders and
welcomes correspondence from those they have been unable to contact.
A Library of Congress record exists under ISBN:23006564

ISBN 13: 978-1-138-55567-9 (hbk)
ISBN 13: 978-1-138-56801-3 (pbk)
ISBN 13: 978-0-203-70536-0 (ebk)

# THE PSYCHOLOGY OF THE CRIMINAL

# THE PSYCHOLOGY OF THE CRIMINAL

BY

M. HAMBLIN SMITH, M.A., M D.

LATE MEDICAL OFFICER OF H.M. PRISON, BIRMINGHAM; LATE LECTURER ON CRIMINOLOGY IN THE UNIVERSITY OF BIRMINGHAM; LECTURER IN CRIMINOLOGY AT BETHLEM ROYAL HOSPITAL, LONDON

SECOND EDITION, REVISED

METHUEN & CO. LTD.
36 ESSEX STREET W.C.
LONDON

*First Published* . . . . *August 31st 1922*
*Second Edition, Revised* . *1933*

PRINTED IN GREAT BRITAIN

# PREFACE

THIS book is based upon twenty-three years' experience in local and convict prisons, and more particularly upon the work which I have done, during the past three years, with offenders from Courts in Birmingham and the adjacent districts.

My main object has been to demonstrate how important is the thorough examination of the individual offender, especially in regard to his mentality. It is only by a great extension of this line of investigation that we can hope to solve the problems which criminality presents.

A considerable part of the book is devoted to that new development of psychology which is known as psycho-analysis, and to the possible applications thereof to the investigation and treatment of offenders. I have included a brief description of the theory and technique of psycho-analysis, so that the reader may not have to look elsewhere for an explanation of technical terms.

There is much in psycho-analysis which is still highly controversial. And it would be quite impossible to write a book on this subject with which all would agree. But I have endeavoured to state fairly and dispassionately the views which I hold. And I do not think that I have made any dogmatic statements which would not be accepted by some eminent exponents of psycho-analysis. To my old friend Dr. G. A. Auden, and to my friend and fellow worker Dr. W. A. Potts, I must express my most hearty thanks for their kindly criticisms of Chapters III and IV, which deal

## vi THE PSYCHOLOGY OF THE CRIMINAL

specially with the psycho-analytic part of my subject. I have made much use of their suggestions. But it is only right to say that they are in no way responsible for the views which I have expressed.

I shall be most pleased to hear from any worker who may see fit to give a trial to the scheme of mental tests described in Chapter II.

I am deeply indebted to my wife for much assistance in revising the proofs.

I have tried to indicate in the book the many sources from which I have derived information. Should I have failed to make proper acknowledgment in any instance, I must crave pardon for such inadvertence. I take this opportunity of expressing the debt which I owe to the work of Dr. William Healy, of Chicago. His great book, "The Individual Delinquent", treats the whole subject of the investigation of offenders as it has never been treated before, and will be found a store-house of information by all who take an interest in this subject.

My thanks are due to the Prison Commissioners, with whose consent this book is published, for permission to use the results of my prison experience in its compilation.

M. HAMBLIN SMITH.

H.M. PRISON, BIRMINGHAM.
*June*, 1922

# PREFACE TO SECOND EDITION

THE demand for a reprint of this book coincides in time with my retirement from the Prison Service and with the termination of my work as Medical Officer of Birmingham Prison.

Changes in the law have necessitated a certain amount of revision. But I have found little in the main thesis of the book which requires alteration. Eleven years additional experience has only served to confirm me in my original view. I am sure that the only hope of solving the problem of delinquency lies in the patient, intensive investigation of the individual offender. So far as psycho-analysis is concerned, I remain a convinced and an unrepentant Freudian.

The publication of the original edition of this book brought me letters of encouragement from all parts of the world, indicating the widely diffused interest in the problems which I have discussed. I desire to express my thanks to these correspondents, most of whom were previously unknown to me.

M. HAMBLIN SMITH.

190, IFFLEY ROAD, OXFORD.
*June*, 1933

# CONTENTS

| CHAPTER | | PAGE |
|---|---|---|
| I. | INTRODUCTORY: THE PROBLEM STATED - | I |
| II. | THE PHYSICAL EXAMINATION OF THE OFFENDER AND THE INVESTIGATION OF THE OFFENDER'S CONSCIOUS MIND - | 27 |
| III. | THE INVESTIGATION OF THE OFFENDER'S UNCONSCIOUS MIND - - - | 64 |
| IV. | THE OFFENDER'S UNCONSCIOUS MIND (*continued*) - - - - | 95 |
| V. | THE VARIOUS CLASSES OF OFFENDERS - | 133 |
| VI. | CONCLUSIONS - - - - | 159 |
| | APPENDIX - - - - - | 179 |
| | INDEX - - - - - | 181 |

viii

# THE PSYCHOLOGY OF
# THE CRIMINAL

### CHAPTER I

## INTRODUCTORY: THE PROBLEM STATED

### I. WHAT WE MEAN BY "CRIMES" AND "CRIMINALS"

THE proper subject of mankind's study is enshrined in an old and trite saying. And yet students of every science which bears in any way upon man have an apparently irresistible tendency to wander from this, their proper goal. It would be impossible to enumerate all the examples of this tendency. But nowhere is it more strongly marked than in the study of offenders. What should be done to offenders has been the subject of much consideration by the makers and administrators of laws from time immemorial. But the fact that they were dealing with individuals seems to have been practically overlooked, until comparatively recent times. Mediaeval theories on this subject are not much in point at the present day, for they were permeated by the predominance of the idea of " free-will " in its most extreme form. It has been well said that the old idea assumed the offender to be in the position of a fig tree which had wilfully and of malice aforethought decided to produce, not figs, but thistles, and that for this most outrageous conduct he naturally deserved condign " punishment ". There is, however, even at the present time, so much

I

## 2 THE PSYCHOLOGY OF THE CRIMINAL

diversity of opinion on the subject of the treatment of offenders that it is necessary to devote a short space to a consideration of what an offender is and of what we mean by " crime ".

Halsbury defines a crime as " an unlawful act or default which is an offence against the public, and which renders the perpetrator of the act or default liable to legal punishment."[1] (Default is, of course, only defect of action or conduct.) The definition of crime in the legal systems of other countries is practically the same as that just given. Some countries have distinctions between different classes of offences. In this country we distinguish between felonies and misdemeanours, and the French code distinguishes between *crime* and *délit*. But with these legal distinctions we are not here concerned.

So crimes are, from the legal point of view, acts which, in the opinion of a particular society, at a particular time, are considered to deserve punishment by that society. Many authorities, Hamon[2] for example, have, of course, used the term in a sense which goes far beyond this. But we are using the term crime (or offence or delinquency) purely in this legal sense. And it follows that, in this sense, a crime is an act which is legally wrong, and which is, essentially, an infringement of the criminal law. The question as to whether the act is " morally " wrong does not come in. Much confusion has been caused by the use of the word " wrong " without explanation of the sense in which it is used. And the single point common to all criminals is that they have committed acts which are considered to deserve punishment by the society in which they live. This fact alone is enough to make us reject, once and for all, the idea that there is anything which can be called a " criminal type ".

[1] " Laws of England," Vol. IX, p. 232.
[2] " The Illusion of Free Will."

## THE PROBLEM STATED 3

Law is a convention which we adopt for the convenience of what we consider to be a well-regulated society. Ultimately, law bases, as do all forms of government, upon force. And the history of the criminal law is the history of the gradual supersession of private vengeance by public vengeance. As courts of law gradually attained power to enforce their decisions, so they gradually took more of the process of vengeance from the private hands in which it had hitherto lain. By a conventional and quite arbitrary distinction, a line of demarcation has been drawn between crimes and " torts ", the latter being wrongs which render the perpetrator subject to the action of the civil, but not of the criminal, law. Our views as to what particular acts should be considered as crimes are constantly, though slowly, changing. Acts which were formerly crimes are so no longer. New crimes have been created by legislatures. The war caused a number of acts to be regarded as crimes, which in pre-war days were not so accounted. And this for the reason that these acts were, in time of war, considered to be prejudicial to the safety of society. And it is a matter of common knowledge, and sometimes of unfavourable comment, that an act may be a crime in one country and not in another. Attempts are sometimes made to avoid the admission that our selection of certain acts as crimes is arbitrary, by describing such acts as " immoral ", " unmoral ", or " non-moral ", or as being " contrary to the eternal principles of right and justice ". But, in reality, such phrases only " darken counsel by words without knowledge ". Eternal principles of right and justice may exist, but our limited intelligences are unable to discover what these principles are. Just as we can only define the position of a point by reference to some other point, so " right " and " wrong", " moral " and " immoral ", are terms whose meaning depends upon some standard. Our standard of morality may

# 4 THE PSYCHOLOGY OF THE CRIMINAL

be one which is set up by some external authority, or it may depend upon the body of tradition handed down from past generations, or it may be the general, average opinion of men of our own time, country, etc. But, however this may be, in any case morality depends upon law, and not law upon morality. And this dependence of morality upon law, upon some standard, requires to be kept in mind.

So much for crimes. And now, since crimes are acts which render their perpetrators liable to legal punishment, we have to consider what " punishment " is.

### II. THE VARIOUS THEORIES OF PUNISHMENT

There are numerous theories of punishment. But, ultimately, they can all be reduced to three, Retaliatory, Deterrent, and Reformatory.

(*a*) Retaliatory punishment is the oldest. " You have hurt me, I will (if I can) hurt you in return " appears to be a fundamental attitude of human nature, and obviously arises from the instinct of self-preservation. In ancient days a man who had injured another man rendered himself liable to vengeance on the part of the injured man (or his family or tribe) if he or they were able to inflict this vengeance. It is most interesting to study the rules laid down for the exaction of vengeance in the Levitical Code. Gradually the conception arose that certain acts were harmful to society, in addition to the injury which they inflicted upon individuals. And the law courts began to take the onus of vengeance from individuals and to administer punishment. Still the idea of retribution was prominent. And this idea seems to be based upon a fundamental instinct of mankind. We have but to watch a child taking his revenge upon some inanimate object against which he has accidentally struck himself to see how primitive this attitude is, and traces of it are even recorded amongst animals

# THE PROBLEM STATED 5

and birds. A man has caused injury to society. And man's sense of " justice " (this being a name for our attempts to rectify the inequalities found in nature) demands that the offender should, in his turn, suffer pain. This idea of retaliation is not popular to-day, and few people will openly admit it. But it is there all the same. And to evade it we are obliged to make "rationalizations", we talk of upholding the majesty of the law, of maintaining the supremacy of society. But even if, as has been suggested, this idea of retaliation is merely a survival of exploded " animistic " doctrines, there is good reason to think that this theory of punishment will have to be reckoned with for many a year to come. Perhaps it may not be desirable that this view of punishment should be entirely overlooked. But there can be no doubt that the effects of this theory have been, and still are, in many ways, evil. To it we owe the determinate, fixed sentence, which still largely obtains, although in some countries matters are now better ordered in this respect. To release an habitual offender at the end of a fixed term, quite irrespective of the effect which his sentence may have produced upon him, can only be justified on this theory of retributive punishment. And the custom of dealing with " petty " offenders by small fines, mingled with occasional short sentences of imprisonment, can only be explained in the same way.

(b) The Deterrent Theory. Many people will say that this is the true object of punishment. A man has injured society. Means must be taken to prevent his doing this again, and to prevent others who might be so inclined from committing similar acts, by making an example of offenders who have been, or are being, punished. It is objected that, upon this theory, we punish a man for acting as he did act, although, according to deterministic doctrine, his action was the only possible action which could have occurred under the

# 6 THE PSYCHOLOGY OF THE CRIMINAL

given circumstances. But this objection does not seem to be valid. The knowledge that he may be punished, that he has previously been punished, that other persons are being or have been punished, for doing a similar act, introduces a new circumstance into the case. The man is not in the same set of circumstances as he would have been had the act not involved the possibility of punishment. The expectation, or anticipation, or recollection of punishment may be sufficient to sway the greater inclination against the performance of some particular act. And so the deterrent theory seems quite compatible with the strictest determinism. We shall never be wholly rid of this theory. And what we have to consider is, not whether punishment may deter, but why it is that, under certain circumstances, it does not deter.

There is a strong objection in many quarters to the use of the word " punishment ". This objection seems valid if by that word we imply simply the infliction of retaliatory pain. But we must not be unduly bound by the tyranny of words. If a man's liberty is in any way restricted by legal authority, against his will, and as a result of any anti-social action on his part, then, ultimately, that is punishment, by whatever name it may be called, or with whatever purpose it may have been inflicted.

(c) The Theory of Reformation. We are inclined, just now, to lay much stress upon this theory. And we have apparently decided that imprisonment is not, *per se*, reformatory. Yet it is an interesting fact that we continue to punish many offences by means of small fines, into which process the idea of reformation cannot possibly enter. It is often said that although punishment may be unpleasant, yet it is necessary that an offender should be punished for the good of society. This argument is really quite beyond the point. If punishment resulted in the good of society, if society

## THE PROBLEM STATED 7

were really improved by the punishment of offenders, then this argument would be unanswerable. But this is just the question at issue. Is society any better for the punishment of an offender, or of any number of offenders? The question is really a serious one. For if the individual is not improved by punishment, and if, at the same time, society is not improved, then the sum total is a loss. We are so accustomed to saying that it is necessary to punish, that we often make no inquiries as to the basis of our process or the results which we expect from it.

The idea of reformatory punishment is comparatively new. In days when the majority of offences were punished by death the notion of reformation could not, of course, come in. It is interesting to remark, in passing, that there was the same vigorous objection to the restriction of capital punishment as that which we hear now from certain sources with reference to modern suggestions of other reform. And the arguments used were practically identical with those of to-day. John Howard is generally regarded as the father of reformatory punishment. But this view seems not quite accurate. He was the father of prison reform, the originator of the modern clean and sanitary prison. But this is quite a different matter. Howard's theory of punishment seems to have been based more on the deterrent idea. He appears to have aimed at preventing a man's return to prison, by making prison a very uncomfortable place by means of silence, solitude, hard work, and absence of all luxuries. In this connexion we must always keep in mind that prison, like any other institution, can never be, at the best, more than a place in which it is possible to prepare for reform. The real test comes on release.

As we said just above, all attempts at reformation will really be punishment, in spite of the scorn which was poured by Mercier and others upon modern reformatory

# 8 THE PSYCHOLOGY OF THE CRIMINAL

penal methods. Much attempt at reformation has been made lately, but it has not been as successful as was at one time expected and hoped. Why is this? The reason is that we have not fully investigated our individual offender. We have made but little attempt to probe into his mind. But in the investigation of the individual offender's mind lies the hope of the future. Other plans have been tried and found wanting. This new plan is seen to be difficult, is seen to involve the abandonment of many cherished superstitions, and so has not been tried. The methods suggested for this most necessary investigation will be fully described and discussed in the next three chapters of this book. We have hitherto been inclined to lay far too much stress on what particular act a man has done, and not nearly enough stress upon what the man is. We shall point out later that conduct is the result of mental life. Any particular act is, at most, only a symptom, and may be quite an unimportant symptom. What we have to do is to discover why a man acts, or has acted, in a particular manner. This involves investigation, and to be of any real value this investigation must be of a thorough and searching character. It is objected by some that the process involved is too elaborate to be applied to small offences. To which we may be permitted to reply, " why small " ? We have really no right to say that any one act is " smaller ", or of less importance than another. " Costs it more pains that what you call a great event should come to pass ? " What is termed a small offence may contain indications of the very first importance.

### III. THE PROBLEM OF RESPONSIBILITY

We can make but little headway in our study of offenders unless we give some attention to this question of " responsibility ". An immense amount of contro-

# THE PROBLEM STATED 9

versy has gathered around this word. And all kinds of theories have been propounded on the subject. The old view, and it is still quite a usual conception, is based upon the metaphysical theory of the " freedom of the will ". It is held, practically, that there is an entity called the " will " which presides over the mind, and which is regarded as the ultimate director of conduct. And it is further held that a man must be required to exercise his will in accordance with certain defined ethical principles. And he is to be accounted as " responsible for his actions ", unless he is incapable (either from mental disease or from mental immaturity) of " knowing right from wrong ". Now this metaphysical theory, in the author's opinion, has no place in any scientific scheme. We cannot, in such a scheme, recognize " will ", apart from individual volitions. The phenomena of volition, like all other natural phenomena, are subject to natural laws. And the phenomena of volition are always caused by their antecedents, heredity, education, and all the factors and influences of previous experiences and environment. (Of course, as we pointed out just now, the remembrance, or the prospect of the possibility, of punishment may be one of the factors in the case.) We cannot think, scientifically, of an uncaused psychical phenomenon, any more than we can think of an uncaused physical phenomenon. And any phenomenon, whether physical or psychical, is the only one which could have been produced by the circumstances of the case. We are therefore obliged to discard this particular theory of responsibility. And we cannot take part in the profitless discussion which has taken place as to what particular degree or kind of mental disease is to be regarded as preventing what Stephen[1] called the " free determination of the will ".

But there is a sense in which we may properly use the word " responsibility ", and in which we may take

[1] " History of the Criminal Law of England ", Vol. II.

# 10 THE PSYCHOLOGY OF THE CRIMINAL

part in scientific discussion on this subject. If we reject the idea that responsibility is something intrinsic to the individual, we may still use the word as expressing the idea of the reaction of society to a given act. If society chooses to decide that under certain special circumstances its normal reaction to some act will be modified, it is, of course, at complete liberty to do so. And society may choose to adopt the rule that certain degrees of mental disease or defect shall materially alter its reaction to acts committed by persons who suffer from such mental disease or defect. We may properly lend our assistance to a Court in order to help it to decide (for the ultimate decision must always lie with the Court) whether such a degree of mental disease or defect exists in any particular case.[1]

The present legal rule on this subject is contained in the answers given by the judges to certain questions put to them by the House of Lords after the trial of McNaughten in 1843. And the gist of this rule is as follows : " That in order to establish a defence on the ground of insanity it must be clearly proved that at the time of committing the act the accused was labouring under such a defect of reason, from disease of the mind, as not to know the nature and quality of the act he was doing, or if he did know it [sic] that he did not know he was doing what was wrong." Very many objections have been taken to this ruling. If the full answers given by the judges are considered, it has been pointed out that they apply to a class of insane persons who do not exist and never have existed. But there are great difficulties in laying down a better definition. Some years ago the Medico-Psychological Association appointed a committee to consider this definition, but this committee failed to produce any improved criterion for use in these cases. In this connexion, it must be remembered that at the time of this committee's action

[1] Rosanoff, " Manual of Psychiatry ".

## THE PROBLEM STATED 11

the "newer psychology" was not yet in existence: nothing was known of psycho-analysis.[1] It may be that in a few years' time it will be possible to produce some improved definition. Meanwhile other attempts have been made in this direction. Balfour Browne gave as a definition of responsibility: "A knowledge that certain acts are permitted by law and that certain acts are contrary to law, and combined with this knowledge the power to appreciate and be moved by the ordinary motives which influence the actions of mankind." Sir James Stephen gave as his opinion that the law is as follows: "No act is a crime if the person who does it is at the time when it is done prevented [either by defective mental power or] by disease affecting his mind: (a) From knowing the nature and quality of his act, or (b) From knowing that the act is wrong, [or (c) From controlling his own conduct, unless the absence of the power of control has been produced by his own default]. But an act may be a crime although the mind of the person who does it is affected by disease, if such disease does not in fact produce upon his mind one or other of the effects above mentioned in reference to that act."[2] Stephen considers that the words enclosed in square brackets are doubtful. The French Penal Code lays down that: "There can be no crime or offence (*délit*) if the accused was in a state of madness at the time of the act." The statutes of the State of New York enact that: "No act done by a person in a state of insanity can be punished as an offence." Both the latter are practical definitions. But it may be objected, what is a state of madness or a state of insanity? Any number of different standards of such states may be set up. Insanity has never been defined legally. And no even tolerable medical definition has ever been given. But we must have some rules. And the present author, very tentatively, proposes as a practical definition as

[1] See Appendix I.  [2] op cit.

## 12 THE PSYCHOLOGY OF THE CRIMINAL

follows : " No act done by a person in a state of insanity, or suffering from mental defect, to such a degree as to justify his being placed under care, treatment, and control, can be punished as an offence." Let us away with disputes about the " knowledge of right and wrong", the " nature and quality of the act ", the " power of self-control ", and the like. The question seems essentially to be this : It is suggested that this accused man is insane or mentally defective. Is his condition such that he should be under care, treatment, and control ? Is he (as it is sometimes put) " certifiably " insane or mentally defective ? The facts which, in the opinion of the medical examiner, indicate such insanity or mental defect would be placed on the medical certificate in the usual way.

Certain objections can be taken to this proposed criterion. Firstly, it will be said that this places the verdict in the hands of the medical expert witnesses. But this is not so. The expert witnesses can only express their opinion, backed by such facts as they are able to allege. A non-criminal lunatic can only be detained in an asylum by a legal order. Truly this order is based upon medical certificates. But each such certificate must rest upon observed facts which are sufficient to justify the physician in signing it. It may or may not contain sufficient evidence of insanity to satisfy the legal authority with whom the detention of the alleged lunatic ultimately rests. Every physician of any experience in the certification of the insane can recall instances in which his certificate has failed to satisfy the legal authority. And so with a Court, under the author's proposed definition.

Secondly, it may be objected that, with this criterion a man may have been regarded as sane until he commits an offence True, but this difficulty occurs with our present tests. Many a murderer has gone about with insanity unsuspected, or not inquired into, until he has

# THE PROBLEM STATED 13

committed the fatal act. Or such a man may have been regarded as being harmless. The author was called as a witness in the case of an imbecile in 1914. The man, although obviously an imbecile, had gone on quietly, and had done a certain amount of useful work, until he, without apparent motive, murdered his sister. We can, after all, only know how a man will act under certain circumstances when those circumstances actually occur. We build a house. It looks perfect on a superficial examination. But the builder has failed to include any arrangements for cooking. The defect is discovered as soon as anyone inhabits the house. There is a kitchen, but no bath. The defect is not discovered until someone who is in the habit of bathing inhabits the house. There is a bath but no fire escape. The defect, in this case, may never be discovered at all.

### IV. THE VARIOUS THEORIES OF CRIMINALITY

The original idea, in this connexion, was that a criminal was a normal man who had yielded to wicked desires from his own " free-will ". While orthodox religious views held the field, the terms wicked and anti-social were taken as synonomous. Charitable persons sometimes took the view " there, but for the grace of God ", etc., but they went no further than that. The whole theory of punishment, so far as any notion of reformation was contained in it, was that the offender had to be persuaded of his " wickedness ". This view is not so prominent to-day. But still the idea which regarded the offender as the constant factor in the problem is very commonly held.

Various theories have been put forward to account for the occurrence of criminality (or delinquency, the term preferred by the author). And these have been termed " general theories ", inasmuch as they take but

# 14 THE PSYCHOLOGY OF THE CRIMINAL

little account of the individual offender. Some of these theories must be glanced at here.

1. Alcohol. The connexion of alcohol with such offences as drunkenness and disorderly conduct, is, of course, not doubted. And what may be termed " crimes of passion " are also often due to alcohol. But whether there is a similar connexion between alcohol and other forms of delinquency is another matter. Alcohol may act as an influence towards delinquency in so many ways. And we have always to consider whether the alcoholism is a primary condition or only a symptom of some underlying mental instability. Again, alcohol often produces poverty, and so produces bad environment, evil companions, opportunities of bad experiences, lack of educational facilities, loss of parental control, disorganization in the home, and quarrelling in the home, this last having far more serious results than is often supposed. In reviewing the case-histories of young delinquents, it is striking to see how many of them come from disorganized homes. The question of parental alcoholism as a cause of delinquency must not be pushed too far, for parents affect their children in many ways apart from heredity. The great experiment now being made in the United States is of vast interest in this connexion. Later, we may be able to estimate its results. At present, it has not been in operation long enough. And the sources from which the statistics of its effects emerge are tainted on both sides by the influence of enthusiasm. But it is a grave question how far the habits of a large proportion of any nation can safely be interfered with by legislative enactment. And it remains to be seen whether other habits will take the place of alcoholism.[1]

2. Bad Environment. 3. Poverty. 4. Bad Heredity. 5. Lack of Education. These may be considered together. There is this difficulty in regarding these things as " causes ", that all persons who have been

[1] See Appendix II.

## THE PROBLEM STATED 15

subjected to them do not become delinquents. So it is clear that there must be some additional cause at work. The majority of people are, comparatively speaking, poor, and come from undesirable environment. Bad heredity often implies poverty and bad environment. It has been found that children with very bad heredity often do well when removed early from bad environment. It is doubtful how far lack of formal education can be considered a cause of delinquency. Poverty may sometimes predispose to offences of a dishonest character.

6. Defective Intelligence. The bearing of mental defect on delinquency will be more fully considered in Chapter V. The question as to what standard (if any) of intelligence may be considered as the " average " for the general population in this country has not yet been determined.

7. Crime has also been considered as a " disease ". There are very strong reasons against using the word disease in this connexion. One of these reasons is that this use of the word implies the existence of some cause acting from without the offender, and so distracts attention from the offender as an individual.

All the above theories tended towards the consideration of the offender as a constant factor in the problem. Lombroso's anatomical theory will be touched on later.

Anyone who commences the study of offenders very quickly finds the weakness of the " general " causation theories. If he starts with the idea that there is a definite " criminal type ", he will soon be undeceived. If, rejecting this view, he proceeds on the assumption that there are a few general classes into which offenders can be divided, he will have to dismiss this idea also. For it will soon be found that the individual offender can only be fitted into these predetermined pigeon-holes by manipulation of the facts. This is the essential weakness of the many attempts which have been made

## 16 THE PSYCHOLOGY OF THE CRIMINAL

to classify offenders under the various headings mentioned above. Each of these general theories of causation has held the field at different times. But no sooner has an enthusiastic worker elaborated one of these systems of classification than others have definitely proved that the system is untenable.

The author is very far from wishing to suggest that each or several of the various general causations just mentioned may not be operative in any particular case. Any one of them, and often more than one, may loom large in the study of some given offender. But the point which the author desires to make is that every case must be studied individually, and that this study must be conducted free from any preconceived theories of causation. The question which we have to solve is this : Why does this particular individual commit anti-social acts ? And no answer can be given to this question unless an honest attempt has been made to investigate the individual's mental constitution.

A Court of justice may take, and has taken, various views of its functions. Far too often it has contented itself by framing and applying what has been well termed " a tariff for crime ". But the true view surely is that a Court is in the position of a prescriber of treatment. Just as a modern physician calls to his aid all the expert assistance which he can obtain, that of the X-ray operator, the bacteriologist, the biochemist, and the like, so no Court can afford to dispense with any of the expert assistance which may be at its disposal. Part of this assistance is the aid of the trained mental examiner. Inquiry into the mental state of offenders is a very specialized matter. And the object of this book is to describe the author's experience in this direction. He trusts that the book may be of interest to all who are engaged in social work. And he ventures to hope that it may be of practical use to three classes of persons (1) Those of his fellow-workers who are

## THE PROBLEM STATED 17

engaged in the study of offenders. (2) Magistrates and others whose daily work lies with offenders, by showing them what may be discovered by mental examination. (3) Social workers, teachers in schools, etc. He also ventures to hope that this book may help, in some small degree, to extend this particular line of research. He believes that no real progress will be made, or is possible, until the system of examination of offenders is greatly extended. Until a Court is in possession of the fullest possible information respecting each case brought before it the work is really being done in the dark. And it is only by skilled examination that the absolutely essential information as to the offender's mental constitution can be obtained.

There are certain points which must be considered at further length.

(a) Recidivism. No words are needed to enforce the importance of this subject. The repeated offender has been the problem and the despair of law-makers and penologists. A glance at any volume of criminal statistics will at once indicate the importance of recidivism. Of those more serious cases which are tried at Assizes and Quarter Sessions it has been calculated that more than seventy per cent. have been previously convicted at least once.

Practically all recidivists commence their delinquent career in early life. The late Dr. C. Goring,[1] in his monumental study, showed, what was already well known to all workers who had investigated the life-histories of offenders, that the majority of recidivists commence their delinquent career between the ages of fifteen and twenty years. And it must be remembered that a first conviction does not, by any means, necessarily imply a first offence. Even in cases which are placed on Probation it very frequently happens that the first appearance in Court only follows on a long series of

[1] " The English Convict."

## 18 THE PSYCHOLOGY OF THE CRIMINAL

offences which have been undetected or undealt with. And it follows that the determining factors of a delinquent life are to be found among the conditions of the offender's early years. (In Chapters III and IV we shall see how this fits in with the theory and the practical findings of psycho-analysis.) Consequently, if these determining factors are to be estimated rightly they must be studied, as far as may be, when they are most active. And they are far clearer in youth than they are in later years. When recidivism has become established various other conditions come into play ; alcoholism, long periods of social disfavour, the establishment of an anti-social grudge, and the ill results of repeated imprisonments. All these conditions render the correct estimation of the fundamental factors in any case much more difficult.

Many of the personal and environmental conditions which tend towards delinquency commence to operate in early life. Knowledge of these conditions is of vast moment, and this knowledge is more easily obtained when the conditions are of recent origin. Let the reader reflect how little he really knows of the early influences which have made him what he is (whatever that may be) and he will partly realize the difficulties of our task.

Once again, youth is the time to investigate offenders, for as years go on there is development of reticence, and of the anti-social feeling, and these render the finding of fundamental conditions to be harder. Psychoanalysis shows us that it is easier to obtain a knowledge of mental conflicts (and these are of vast importance) at a time when the subject has not to probe too deeply for these conflicts, and when succeeding experiences have not buried the complex resulting from the conflict so completely.

Yet once more, all those who take a part in any schemes for the reformation of offenders feel rightly

## THE PROBLEM STATED 19

that the case is far more hopeful when taken in hand young. To see the truth of this we have only to compare our feelings when dealing with young prisoners and with old convicts.

But although we have laid much stress on the predominant need for the careful study of commencing delinquency, we must not depreciate the importance of work with the older offenders. The intensive examination of the younger cases tends to a fuller comprehension of the needs of the older cases. Knowledge of the causative factors which are, as just explained, most easily ascertained among the young, will lead to better diagnosis and treatment of offenders of every age, however long may have been their delinquent careers. When considering an older offender we must try, as far as may be, to ascertain what were the factors which operated at the start of his delinquent course. Thus, careful study of these factors will help us with every class of offender. We may often be unable to ascertain all the factors in a given case. But the investigation is always useful, always should be made, so long as we remember that it is necessary to avoid any hasty diagnosis, any rapid attempt to classify our case. Study of cases will not always ensure success in the definite assignment of the important factor or factors of causation. We shall generally find that diagnosis implies the careful weighing and estimation of a number of factors.

There is one marked difference between the recidivist and the man who has committed a single offence (always keeping in mind the warning that a first conviction does not necessarily imply a first offence). The man who has committed a single, non-repeated offence has found some reason for the non-repetition. Penologists are entitled to make what they can of the argument that the punishment awarded is the reason for this non-repetition. Doubtless it is so in some cases. Or the particular circumstances which produced the

## 20 THE PSYCHOLOGY OF THE CRIMINAL

offence may not recur. An offence may be committed in some sudden access of passion, and the occasion of this may have been unique. A mental conflict may result on one occasion in an offence, and may not issue into action in this way again.

(b) There are delinquents who do not come within the purview of the Courts at all. This is, of course, no new knowledge to any person of experience. But the author has had most interesting confirmation of this fact in his work. A certain amount of newspaper publicity naturally accrues to Court work. And he has found himself consulted, sometimes personally, sometimes by letter, by people who have difficult cases on their hands. Such cases are usually those of young boys or girls, though sometimes of older persons, who are a trouble to their relatives on account of their repeated offences. Sometimes these offences are those of dishonesty, of stealing from their affectionate relations who have to deal with the matter without the aid of the law, sometimes of stealing from others who have been placated or recompensed by the relations, and so have not brought the matter before the Courts. In other cases the delinquency has taken other forms. The author has been unable, from lack of time and other reasons, to deal with these cases otherwise than by general advice. But he has sometimes been able to suggest that the advice and treatment of a fellow-worker should be obtained, and, in certain instances, the results have been excellent. These cases are by no means infrequent, and they may be appallingly sad. There is a great opening for work in this direction. And as the science of psycho-analysis grows, it may be hoped that there will be an increase in the number of persons with skill, experience, and discretion, who will be ready to undertake the treatment of such cases, and so to diminish the amount of sadness in the world.

(c) Throughout this book the author has avoided

## THE PROBLEM STATED 21

the use of the words " sin " and " vice ". Without entering into highly controversial matters, it must be clear that the use of these words implies the adoption of some more or less arbitrary standard. We have only to read old books on penology to see the confusion which resulted from regarding offenders as " sinners ". This view is not so much in vogue now. But, in any case, we must not introduce it into a scientific investigation. We have " no need of that hypothesis ". Apart from the fact that many " sins " which are not punished by the criminal law may have results far more dire and far-reaching than certain offences which are so punished, there is this other consideration. The great question is not so much what a man has done, but what he is. We shall lay down the fundamental position that conduct is the direct result of mental life, that misconduct, like all other forms of conduct, results from mental causes. The particular act with which a man is charged in Court is only a symptom produced by these mental causes. Groszman [1] puts it well, when he says— " For every symptom we must train ourselves to look for a cause. Proper observation implies a careful distinction between facts observed and the interpretation we may give them. It is a common error to substitute our interpretation of a fact for the fact itself ". And he illustrates the principle in this way—" To say that to-day the child was naughty means nothing. Such a statement implies a foregone conclusion, a judgment, not a record of fact, unless of the fact that the child's conduct affected the recorder in a certain manner ". It follows that the real question is not so much what should be done to an offender in the way of punishment, but what can be done for him in the way of treatment.

The first great advance in the study of the offender was made by Lombroso and his disciples. He was the

[1] " The Exceptional Child."

## 22 THE PSYCHOLOGY OF THE CRIMINAL

founder of what may be called the "anatomical" school of criminology. His conception of the offender was based upon generalizations (perhaps unwise) which were derived from premisses far too small. Many of his conclusions are now considered to be erroneous. There is much in his theory of the offender as being an "atavistic" survival, which is confirmed by the researches of psycho-analysis. But his theory of the relation between epilepsy and delinquency is now generally abandoned, and was only tenable by giving a very extended meaning to the term epilepsy. The fact, however, that his theories have had to be revised, in no way detracts from the value of the service which he rendered to science, and so to the world. For in Lombroso's work, one great principle transcends all the details which he gathered. His great glory lies in his insistence on the fact, practically overlooked before his time, that the offender is to be studied in himself, as an individual, and apart from any particular offence with which he might happen to be charged. Like Columbus, Lombroso did not rightly recognize the country which he had discovered. His followers, perhaps, find no feature in his maps which can stand uncorrected. His undying fame rests on the fact that he did lead us to a new country, and opened out a new field for our explorations.

We do not now talk of a "criminal type" of cranium or ear. We recognize the "stigmata of degeneration", as they are called. We know them to be common among offenders. But it is now understood that they have no special relation to the offender as such, in no way differentiate him from the non-offender, and are common among our delinquents, simply because many delinquents are defective or subnormal mentally. All facts are, of course, worthy of study. And we do well to measure heads and ears, so long as we recognize that such abnormalities are not in themselves causes

# THE PROBLEM STATED 23

of delinquency, any more than are an offender's nationality or his religious faith.

## V. THE RISE OF THE PSYCHOLOGICAL VIEW.

From whence then, comes the light upon the stony road which we have to travel ? The answer is, From Psychology. This, the youngest of the sciences, was engaged for many years in the study of academic problems, and was not much concerned with matters of ordinary life. Psychology was reproached with its aloofness from the affairs of the world. But the seclusion of this science was well. For in this seclusion it was studying its methods and perfecting its technique. We must not say learning its limitations. For in its own sphere it has no limitations. Human psychology may, from one point of view, be regarded as the science which investigates human conduct. No nobler study can be conceived. Conduct is the direct result of mental life. None of the causes of delinquency just enumerated can have any effect in this direction except in so far as they affect mental life. Psychology studies human conduct, and the mental elements which produce human conduct, the motives of human conduct in the individual and in the mass. It studies these in the " normal ", the " average " individual, and then proceeds to the study of them in the pathological, the diseased. This leads directly to the view that the offender must be studied as an individual, and that he must be regarded, not as a constant, but as the most variable element in the problem.

Psychology has now emerged from the gloom, and stands ready, with the other sciences, to assist mankind in its struggles. The value of the study of the " conscious " mind has long been known. Various methods of mental testing, to be described in some detail in the next chapter, have proved to be of the greatest service

## 24 THE PSYCHOLOGY OF THE CRIMINAL

in the unravelling of some problems in delinquency. But we should still have been groping in the dark had it not been for the latest achievement of psychology, the hypothesis of the " unconscious mind ", and the methods of its investigation. This, the greatest achievement of modern times, perhaps of all times, will be dealt with, after an elementary fashion, in Chapters III and IV.

The dependence of conduct upon mental life has, of course, long been recognized in certain practical bearings, although its basis is only just beginning to be investigated. The demagogic politician, the popular newspaper, the religious leader, the advertising agent, have long made use of this dependence. We now claim that the science of psychology indicates the road which we must follow in our study of delinquents, the only road which we can follow with the hope of attaining ultimate peace, because the only road which leads us to the study of what the delinquent really is.

If we consider for a moment the immediate antecedents of any example of delinquency, we see at once how intimately related are conduct and mental life. One man kills another, and the action was the result of the emotion of anger produced by what the victim had said or done. Or, again, in a burglary the action was the result of a deliberately formed mental plan. Or, yet again, a man has yielded to some sudden impulse which prompted him to the gratification of some desire. So it is abundantly clear that the one way to investigate the causes of an offence is to ascertain, as far as may be done, the mental processes which have produced the delinquent action. To overlook this mental factor, is a sure way to the formation of erroneous conclusions. It is thus that the general causation theories have led to so much misapprehension. This is why the easy " explanation " of assigning some external cause for delinquency has led so often to mistaken conclusions.

# THE PROBLEM STATED 25

The subject may be an alcoholic, yet the real cause of his delinquency may be congenital mental defect. The subject's environment or his family-history may have been hopelessly bad, but the true cause of his delinquency was some buried mental conflict. Here we see the true solution of the problem often put to us, Why is it that of a number of persons in a given environment, or with a particular family-history, or of similar habits, one or more become delinquent, while the rest do not so become ? We have but to consider this, to reject, once and for all, the " general " theories of crime. These easy " explanations " have drawn us from our true goal, the study of the individual. It has been well said " savages explain, science investigates ".

And so, although we must deeply respect the work of Lombroso and his followers, who first grasped the necessity of the study of the delinquent as an individual, we see why it was that their work led to such inadequate results. They failed to see that it is needful to investigate the mind of the offender, and to ascertain what are the immediate mental mechanisms which produced his delinquency. The social and biological causes which assist in the production of delinquency are of great importance, and we must not underrate them. They are worthy of deep study, and they should, if possible, be amended. But they are of quite secondary importance, as compared with the study of the mental mechanisms of the individual. We can only arrive at a correct diagnosis by means of this study of mental mechanisms, and this study is also the surest line to devising correct methods of treatment.

This particular study of the individual is the main theme of this book. We shall, in the next chapter, consider the investigation of the offender's conscious mind. And in Chapters III and IV we shall deal with the investigation of the unconscious mind. This latter study, still in its infancy, is, in the author's opinion,

3

## 26  THE PSYCHOLOGY OF THE CRIMINAL

the key to the whole position.   In Chapter V we shall
see how our findings can help us to understand various
classes of offenders.   And we shall, in Chapter VI,
conclude with some reflections upon the way in which
our findings affect our estimation of delinquents, and
how they should, and will, affect our views on the
treatment of delinquency.

CHAPTER II

## THE PHYSICAL EXAMINATION OF THE OFFENDER AND THE INVESTIGATION OF THE OFFENDER'S CONSCIOUS MIND

LET us take it that we have our offender before us, and that we have commenced our investigation by making a full and complete physical examination. The absolute necessity of this examination need not be laboured. It is not necessary to point out how certain physical defects may be very strong incentives towards delinquency. Tuberculosis, heart disease, hernia, defects of vision, etc., may all be, in a sense, " causes " of delinquency, inasmuch as they prevent, or tend to prevent, the sufferer from earning a living in the ordinary labour market. Various statistical investigations of the incidence of defects of this kind among the delinquent population have been made. But they are inclined to be misleading, because we have no reliable statistics of the incidence of these disabilities among the ordinary population. And, further, the delinquent population must not, in fairness, be compared with the general population, and we do not know with what section (if with any) of the population the delinquent may be compared. We have had, for example, researches which have proved that the offender is peculiarly insensitive to pain, and similar researches which appear to have the opposite result, these discrepances being due to the class with which the

## 28 THE PSYCHOLOGY OF THE CRIMINAL

offenders examined have been compared. All the same, there can be no doubt that physical disabilities are of importance in the production of delinquency. And they should be, if possible, remedied. Visual defects should be corrected by suitable spectacles. Herniæ should be fitted with trusses, and in suitable cases a radical cure could be done. In an ideal state all this would be done as a matter of course. And there is one other point of importance. The amount of dental disease among delinquents is very large. The author does not suggest that it is larger than in the case of the general population, but it is admitted that the teeth of the nation urgently require attention. And we might well make a start with the inmates of our institutions, offenders included, they being under conditions in which dental attention could be easily provided. There is but little doubt that the irritability produced by certain physical disabilities (carious teeth, nasal obstruction, etc.) may be potent causes in the production of juvenile delinquency.

In considering the evil effects of bad physical conditions, we must remember that it is not only the effect upon the sufferer's working powers which has to be taken into account. The matter goes deeper, and may start earlier than would be accounted for in that way. Take the case of a boy with very defective vision. The defect may not be known to anyone. But the boy will not be able to do his work at school. Consequently he may be in constant trouble with his teachers, and may be rebuked and punished for carelessness, inattention, and stupidity. Ignorant of the real cause of his trouble, and conscious that he has been doing his best, a mental conflict will be established. With our modern system of school medical inspection such cases are now discovered and rectified. But it is likely that a delinquent career in many older offenders may have been started in just this way. The same considera-

## THE OFFENDER'S CONSCIOUS MIND 29

tions hold good in cases of deafness, enlarged tonsils, adenoids, etc.

Again, all who have studied the question must see that early formation of good habits of industry, etc. is of the first importance as a preventive of delinquency. Now the physically defective boy or girl is handicapped in this direction. The phthisical or cardiac case is unable to work regularly. The physically weak child is often kept away from school. Bad habits are thus formed early. These cases, naturally, receive an extra amount of sympathy from their friends, and they come to demand this. Thus there is produced a decided predisposition to neurotic troubles.

Defect of the power of sense perception in any direction is always an indication for very thorough examination. As we have just shown, it may be, in itself a predisposing cause for delinquency. Or it may be an indication of general mental deficiency. Some observers have stated that the mentally defective often have an abnormally keen sense of smell. If this statement is correct it indicates reversion to a primitive type. It is a matter of common experience that olfactory sensations are particularly prone to revive old memories from the unconcious. It is a strange fact that olfactory sensations are very uncommon in dreams.

In all our considerations as to the numbers of physically or mentally defective delinquents whom we meet with, as compared with more normal delinquents, we must keep in mind the fact that such defective offenders are more likely to be detected and arrested than are more normal offenders.

Certain physical disabilities act in another way also. They tend to make their possessor anti-social because they induce him to regard himself as different to other men. Epilepsy, and severe impediments in speech may be specially mentioned in this connexion. And the subject will be taken up at greater length in Chapter V.

## 30 THE PSYCHOLOGY OF THE CRIMINAL

It is proper to mention here that much evidence is being collected upon the influence of certain bodily organs, known as the " ductless glands " (the thyroid and thymus glands, and others) not only upon physical health, but also upon mental health, and, as a result, upon conduct. Cretinism, due to congenital defect of the thyroid gland, is an example. Much work is being done upon the investigation and possible cure of the conditions produced by the abnormalities of these glands. It is likely, in time, that the results obtained by workers in this particular field will have a considerable effect upon our conceptions of some forms of delinquency. But we cannot, as yet, make any definite statement on this subject.

All those who have studied Lombroso's works, and those of some of his followers, are aware of the importance these writers attach to the presence of certain physical abnormalities of the cranium, palate, ear, hair, etc., these being known as the " stigmata of degeneration." Abnormalities in the shape or size of the cranium may imply the presence of abnormalities in the brain. And these, as well as the other stigmata, indicate either incomplete development or a tendency to reversion to a more primitive type. Although the importance attached to these stigmata is not so great as formerly, and although we no longer hold the exaggerated views which were held by certain of Lombroso's earlier disciples, still the stigmata are of some moment, more especially from the point of view of prognosis. It may be supposed that in a person whose mind does not function properly there is either inferiority of structure or function of the brain. And since the brain itself is not within our purview, we have to content ourselves by estimating its condition by that of the parts of the body which we are able to investigate. The stigmata suggest that the other parts of the body are inferior—although superiority in one organ may compensate for deficiency

## THE OFFENDER'S CONSCIOUS MIND 31

in another organ. And when we are asked as to the prospects of improvement or cure in any given case, we must not overlook the presence of these stigmata.

It has been said that the offender is a person of poor physique. It is true that he often is. But so are many of the other members of that social class from which the offender comes. The matter is well summed up by Goring when he says : " The physical and mental constitution of both criminal and law-abiding persons of the same age, class, stature and intelligence, are identical ".[1] And some statistics which the present author collected, with regard to the relation between the height and weight of 3,000 unselected convicts, completely agreed with Goring's view.

We must now proceed to the investigation of the offender's mind. This is of even greater importance than the investigation of his physical condition, for we have pointed out how conduct is the direct result of mental life. In this chapter we shall consider the investigation of the offender's " conscious " mind. And by this phrase we mean that part of his mind which can be reached by " ordinary " methods, that is to say, without the aid of the newer methods of psycho-analysis.

We have first to eliminate any definite " insanity ". Cases of insanity are dealt with in one of two ways. In serious charges the question is investigated at the trial. Medical evidence is called, and the jury are at liberty to return a verdict of " guilty, but insane at the time of commission of the act " ; or they may find the prisoner " insane on arraignment", i.e., that, on account of mental disease, he is unfit to be tried at all. In either case the order of the Court is the same. The prisoner is directed to be detained " until His Majesty's pleasure shall be known ", and removal to an asylum follows. This procedure can only be used at Courts of Assize or Quarter Sessions. But in the case of a charge of a

[1] " The English Convict ", p. 370

## 32 THE PSYCHOLOGY OF THE CRIMINAL

less serious nature the offender is remanded to the Prison for medical examination and report. If he is found to be certifiably insane, the Court is so informed. The offender is certified at the Court, removed direct to an asylum, and the case goes no further. The question as to whether an offender should be certified as insane does not differ, essentially, from similar problems in ordinary practice. So we need say no more on this head.

We are now confronted by a more difficult matter. The delinquent conduct, for which the offender comes within the purview of the Court, is the direct result of his mental life. And so we have to attempt an investigation of his mental constitution, his " mental make-up ". This question should really be considered in every case. Our arrangements are not yet adequate for this. So, in the majority of cases, such investigation is confined to offenders who are specially remanded for this inquiry, and to certain other cases of youthful offenders.

We have said, in the last chapter, that psychology is the youngest of the sciences. Applied psychology is still younger, and one of its more recent developments is the study of mental processes by the use of " tests ". In the application and interpretation of these mental tests there are difficulties to be overcome and fallacies to be avoided. A short experience of their use will quickly demonstrate these. And this is not the place to enter into discussion of the many practical and theoretical objections which can be raised against any particular test. But to learn anything about the condition of the offender's conscious mind we must make use of tests. Every question which is put to an offender, or any observation made upon him, is, in a sense, a " test ". But for convenience it is necessary to have some scheme of tests for routine use. And it will be found that every worker, however much he may be disposed to depreciate the use of tests, is really working with some scheme of his

# THE OFFENDER'S CONSCIOUS MIND    33

own. There are a number of standard schemes in use; some good for one purpose, and some for another. Perhaps the one best known in this country is the original Binet scale, and its various modifications, especially that devised by Lewis M. Terman, of the Leland Stanford Junior University.[1] This will be referred to in this chapter as the " Terman scheme ". These schemes were originally devised for the examination of school children. And for use with these, and for other offenders up to the age of about 18 years, the author has found them to be fairly satisfactory. These schemes depend upon the principle laid down by Binet, and confirmed in its general features by many succeeding workers, that there is, normally, a regular development of intelligence as age progresses, and that there is a definite standard for each age, to which standard a normal child may be expected to conform. Whether this development continues throughout life, or whether, as some appear to suggest, there is a halt at the age of 18 years, is a debated question. The Binet scheme was originally arranged for French school children, and the Terman scheme for American children, and this must not be forgotten.

For work in Children's Courts these schemes would, no doubt, be excellent. But the author, in his Court work, deals with no children under 16 years, and with comparatively few offenders between the ages of 16 and 18 years. And he required a scheme which could be used for adolescents and others. He has employed tests on subjects of all ages, from 6 to 80 years. But he has come to the conclusion that, as a rule, persons over the age of 30 years do not react well to formal schemes of tests, and that the results of tests derived from such subjects are misleading. There are exceptions to this rule, especially among the older low-grade mental defectives.

The author has made use of tests for about 25 years. His earlier work was done with the Binet scheme,

[1] " The Measurement of Intelligence."

## 34 THE PSYCHOLOGY OF THE CRIMINAL

as was the case with most workers in this line. But, for reasons which will be set out shortly, he has formed the conclusion that the Binet scheme was not well suited to his purpose. Healy's scheme, as used by that worker at Chicago, is also well known and is most excellent. It has the disadvantage of being somewhat lengthy, and there is at present no special guide to its use, Healy's monograph on the subject being out of print.[1] There are also other schemes, some of which will be mentioned later.

Any scheme has to be judged not merely as a whole but in respect to its individual tests ; and the author has formed very definite views as to what a test should and should not be. To his mind a satisfactory test must comply with the following conditions :

1. It must be capable of arousing at least moderate interest, for the co-operation of the subject is absolutely essential.

2. It must be free from any undue appearance of childishness. It must not be unduly easy, for such tests only arouse resentment on the part of the subject. And it must not be " tricky " or suggest the idea of a riddle.

3. The idea of the test must be fairly easy to grasp, and must not require too much explanation. Some of the Terman tests are very defective in this, the most important requirement of all. If too much explanation is given, the test is spoiled. But with many of the Terman tests it is always a matter of uncertainty whether the subject understands what he is required to do. Mental testing is so important, and the results in Court work may be so serious, that we must feel absolutely safe about the value of the results obtained from the tests.

4. A scheme of tests must contain definite tests to estimate the results of the subject's formal school

[1] Although there is a description of many of the tests in Healy's Book " The Individual Delinquent ".

# THE OFFENDER'S CONSCIOUS MIND 85

education. But the bulk of the tests should be independent of this factor.

5. The scheme must not be unduly favourable to a certain class of defectives known as the "verbalist" type. The precise meaning of this phrase, first applied by Healy, will be explained in Chapter V. The Terman scheme is defective in this respect; far too many of the tests depending upon ability in the use of language.

6. Tests should be capable, as far as possible, of interpretation in terms of definite mental processes. And a scheme should present tests for a fair number of these processes.

Failure to comply with one or more of these conditions has led the author to eliminate the majority of the Terman tests.

A scheme was wanted which would be suitable to the ages mentioned previously. And another requirement was a scheme which would normally occupy not more than 45 minutes. Apart from other reasons, the average subject cannot stand more than this without showing signs of fatigue, and so vitiating the results of the examination. After prolonged experimentation, and the trying of many tests, the author has arranged the following scheme, which he is, at present, using for all his cases which appear suitable for formal testing. It is as follows :—

1. *Reading*. The subject is given a card on which is printed a passage relating to a fire, and containing about 130 short and ordinary words. He is told to read this aloud (if he is unable to read, it is read to him). His manner of reading and the comprehension which he appears to show of the passage is noted. The card is then removed, and he is asked to repeat as much of the passage as he can recall, being told that the sense only is wanted and that he may use his own words. The number of such "memories" and the order in which they are recalled is noted.

## 36 THE PSYCHOLOGY OF THE CRIMINAL

2. *Writing.* A few dictated words are given. The phrase, " I saw the dog run after the cat ", is generally made use of, because of the peculiar inclination of mental defectives to write, " I was the god ".

3. *Arithmetic.* The simple multiplication sum 25 × 35 is given on paper. The method of working and the result obtained are noted. Of course, if a subject makes a gross error in the result, and fails to see this when it is pointed out to him, that is evidence of defect of reasoning power. This sum is followed by the simple mental problem " If you can buy two eggs for fivepence, how many eggs can you buy for fifty pence ? " Nearly all defectives fail at this, but so do a number of non-defectives. After this the question is asked : " If you go for a ride on a car, and the fare is twopence halfpenny, how much change should the conductor give you out of a two shilling piece ? " It is a most interesting fact that this is nearly always answered correctly, even by the mentally defective. It is, of course, an example of the kind of problem which must be solved if a subject is to live at all in the ordinary world. The results on these first three tests are compared with the standard (if known) attained by the subject at school, often giving an interesting light upon the advantage of having passed some particular standard. But no special stress is laid upon these tests in making a diagnosis of mental defect, except as regards the problem about the change. The position attained at school is not, in itself, any safe measure of intellectual capacity. It is, at most, an artificial standard based upon efficiency in certain limited directions. It may be argued that, if we know a subject to have attended school for several years, and not be able to do such elementary work as that just outlined, the fact is in itself indicative of mental defect. But we must be very cautious in drawing this conclusion. We must remember the vast differences which exist in efficiency of teaching. And we must also remember the

# THE OFFENDER'S CONSCIOUS MIND 37

small use which is made in after-school life, by the class from which most offenders are drawn, of the subjects of school education. If a man who had certainly received a superior education was unable to do these tests, that would be very strong evidence of some mental trouble. But many readers of this book might not care to have such matters of their own school-days as " square root " or " practice " suddenly tested, to say nothing of algebra.

The educational tests can be extended to any desired degree, and it is sometimes useful to do this. The remainder of the tests in this scheme are practically independent of formal education.

4. *The " Memory Span "* for a series of numerals, increasing in number from four to eight and read at the rate of one per second, is tested, the subject being given a second trial if he fails at the first series presented, but no second trial at the others. The average for non-defectives is six numerals, but defectives very seldom attain to this.

5. *First Form Board.* This is the board originally described by Healy. It is included in the Terman scheme. The board consists of a rectangular frame, into which fit exactly five rectangular blocks. It can easily be constructed by anyone with a little mechanical ability. This test is usually done quickly by non-defectives, and about 50 per cent. of defectives do it also.

6. *Second Form Board.* This is rather more difficult and is similar to Healy's test of the same name, with one modification. In Healy's board the pieces are interchangeable, in the author's certain of the pieces are not so. This has an advantage. The subject is carefully instructed before he begins the test that all the pieces will fit in easily if he gets them into the proper places. If, after this instruction, he still persists in trying to crowd a piece into a space which it will not fit, it is clear that he does not comprehend a simple direction. This

## 88 THE PSYCHOLOGY OF THE CRIMINAL

test is done by the great majority of non-defectives. Only about 33 per cent of defectives are able to manage it.

Both form boards are tests of attention, perseverance, and the ability to plan a simple piece of work. There are two methods of doing them. The ideal method, of course, is to consider the problem first, and then to attempt it. This plan is sometimes adopted. But the more usual way is to try various solutions, and to discard those which prove impossible. The ability to profit from our errors is a decidedly valuable mental trait. Constant repetition of obvious absurdities is very characteristic of the defectives' attempts at these two tests. And another thing often tried by this class of subject, with the first board, is to get all the pieces in save one ; and then to try a similar arrangement placing the pieces at the other end of the board ; and to get so far that only one step is required and then to stick completely, is a third result often seen with defectives. The time taken with either board is not considered, but a markedly slow or quick solution is noted ; and the same remark holds good for all the other tests. A slow but planful solution may be much more meritorious than a more rapid result by trial and error. And, moreover, with the first board there is a distinct possibility of hitting on the correct solution by chance. Terman requires the subject to perform the first board three times in five minutes. To keep a subject doing the same test more than once is quite contrary to the author's ideas. With a failure on either board, it is well to demonstrate to the subject that the test is quite an easy one.

7. " *Aussage* " or *Testimony Test*. The subject is told to look carefully at a brightly coloured picture of a butcher's shop, being warned that he will be questioned upon what he has observed. About twenty seconds is allowed for this examination. The picture is then placed out of sight. And the subject is told to give a

# THE OFFENDER'S CONSCIOUS MIND   89

free description of what he has observed.   When he has
told all that he remembers, he is examined upon details
omitted by him in free description.   The results are
noted, the free description being classed as " dramatic ",
good, fair, poor, or bad.   Opportunity is taken of questioning the subject upon details which are not in the
picture.   The test is one of attention, observation, and
suggestibility.   The last point is of considerable importance with the delinquent class.   But it is only fair to
state that subjects who might appear, from their history,
etc., to be highly suggestible, do not always show this
on their test performance.   Defectives seldom do better
than " poor " on free description, and they show distinctly more evidence of suggestibility than do non-
defectives.   Healy's standard picture is used, but there
is no special reason for this, any suitable coloured picture
would do.

8.   *Interpretation of Pictures.*   Two of the pictures in
the Terman scheme are used (*a*) The Colonial Home,
which shows a woman weeping, and a dejected looking
man leaving the room.   (*b*) The Post Office, which shows
a number of laughing farmers listening to one of their
number reading from the newspaper.   A mere enumera-
tion of the objects in the picture is counted as a failure.
For success, a subject is required to bring out some sensible idea which the picture suggests to him.   For
instance, the following solutions have been counted as
successful in the first picture (the correct answer being
that there has been a quarrel) : (1) The man has been
knocking the woman about.   (2) The man has brought
bad news.   (3) The man is leaving for the war.
(4) There has been impropriety between the man and
the woman.   (5) The parting of Napoleon and Josephine,
sometimes given by those who have seen the popular
play " A Royal Divorce ".   With the second picture
the subject is required to bring out the point that the
man is reading good or amusing news.   Sometimes this

# 40 THE PSYCHOLOGY OF THE CRIMINAL

result is only obtained after questioning the subject : this is counted as a half success. This second picture is, perhaps, not quite so satisfactory as it might be, and the author will be grateful to any reader who can suggest a better picture for the test.

9. *Comparison of the lengths*, first of three pairs of unequal lines, the longer being in each case on the right hand side, and then of the lengths of three pairs of equal lines. The test was in the original Binet scheme, and is of value. It is one of suggestibility. There is no marked difference between the results obtained from defectives and non-defectives, although the former are more likely to accept the suggestions. Some subjects fail to recognize the inequality in the lines of one or more of the first three pairs.

10. *Reproduction on Paper of Two Designs*, shown together for 10 seconds. This also was in the original Binet scheme. Here again there is no great difference shown as between defectives and non-defectives. The author scores the test more leniently than Terman allows.

11. *Terman's Cricket Ball Test.* A circle of about $2\frac{1}{2}$ inches diameter represents a round grass field, a small gap being left in the circumference to represent the gate. The subject is given a pencil, and is told that he is to suppose that he has lost a ball (or for girls a purse) in the field ; that, except that it is in the field, he does not know at all where it is ; that he is to consider the problem and to trace out what would be the best path to take in order to make sure of finding the lost article. The result may be a superior plan, an inferior plan, or no plan at all. Very few defectives produce anything which can possibly be called a plan, and when they do produce one it is nearly always inferior. Of non-defectives more than fifty per cent. produce a superior plan, and very few fail to produce some kind of plan. The test is an excellent one. It brings out, *inter alia*, the ability to

# THE OFFENDER'S CONSCIOUS MIND   41

grasp the essentials of a given situation, to comprehend simple directions, and to plan a piece of work.

12. *Cancellation.* This is the well-known task of erasing from a sheet of mixed capital letters all the specimens of one particular letter. It is a test of attention. The method adopted is interesting to watch. Most subjects adopt the natural plan of going along each line in succession ; but some of the defectives dodge about the sheet in an apparently purposeless manner. A normal person should feel quite certain of the accuracy of his first attempt. But we meet with subjects who will go over the sheet twice, and, if allowed, more often still.

13. *Continuous Subtraction.* The problem of subtracting from 100 by successive 7's is first given. If the subject fails at that he is given the task of subtracting from 31 by successive 3's. If he still fails he may be tried at counting backwards from 20, as in the original Binet scheme. The test is one of attention, and of control of mental processes. Very few defectives can do the 3's ; only one, in the author's experience, has been found to do the 7's. On the other hand, the great majority of non-defectives do 3's or better.

14. *Heilbronner's Apperception Test.* This consists of a series of sets of cards, each successive card in the set showing rather more detail in the representation of some common object (lamp, bicycle, etc.), until the complete object is shown in the final card. Of the fourteen sets in Heilbronner's original test, four have been rejected as being unfamiliar to English subjects. The cards in each set are presented in their order, and a note is made of the point at which the subject names correctly the object shown. Scoring is done on very generous lines, a success being counted if the subject recognizes the object when not more than half the detail has been exhibited. This test is of much interest, and will prove of value. But the results are, as yet, too few to justify any very definite statements on the matter. So far,

4

# 42 THE PSYCHOLOGY OF THE CRIMINAL

however, there does not seem to be any very marked difference between the defectives and others as concerns this test. It is not uncommon to find a defective whose powers of apperception, tested in this way, are quite good. There is sometimes a trace of suggestibility to be observed in using this test. Two of the objects are a pen and a pencil. The subject having named the pen correctly, sometimes calls the pencil a pen also.

15. *Healy's Pictorial Completion Test.*[1] This is rather difficult to describe. It consists of a brightly coloured picture, mounted on wood, and in which ten 1-inch squares have been cut out. The subject is given the picture and 45 blocks, each 1-inch square, of which 40 bear a representation of some object, while the other 5 are blanks. He is required to fill in the picture with the blocks which, in his opinion, make the best sense. Care is taken to see that he thoroughly understands what he has to do by means of the demonstration of the correct filling of one space by the examiner. The subject is then left to complete the picture by himself A note is made of final errors, " logical " and " illogical ", the latter being errors for which the subject can give no reasonable explanation. No words are adequate to express the value of this test. It is as nearly perfect a test for mental defect as we have. A complete success in doing this test is almost definite disproof of mental defect. The author has, however, had one case of undoubted mental defect which did attain complete success at this test. The way in which the subject approaches the problem is most interesting to watch. Mental control and association processes are well brought out, the latter by questioning the subject on his final errors. The advantage of learning all we can on these points, when dealing with delinquents, is obvious. The author began to use this test with much hesitation, as he feared that his subjects might regard it

[1] " The Psychological Review ", May, 1914.

# THE OFFENDER'S CONSCIOUS MIND    43

as childish and resent its exhibition. Experience has proved that this fear was quite groundless ; subjects take the greatest interest in the problem. The only drawback to the test is that it is decidedly expensive.[1]

18.[2] *Test as to General Information and Interests.* Questions of this kind are rightly included in most schemes of mental tests. But there is not, and perhaps cannot, be any general agreement as to what may be regarded as the average range of information. The author began to work with Healy's standard *questionnaire,* modified as required for English conditions. But he soon had to give this up, for some of the questions were found altogether too difficult. His main perplexity is that his work is confined to offenders. And it is not clear to what class, if any, of the outside population offenders can properly be compared. Questions such as the manner of working of a steam engine or a motor car are quite out of place with the majority of offenders. And one may perhaps ask what class of persons, apart from engineers, could usually give any definite information on these points. We sometimes find a boy who is able to give a general idea of the processes involved, and he turns out to have a marked mechanical interest : but such cases are very rare. The author is in the habit of asking the following questions, or a selection from them. Where intelligent interest is shown, the questions can be expanded to any desired degree. The answers he records are simply the general type of answers obtained in examination, and they are not the answers got from the mentally defective class in particular. Among these latter every possible degree of ignorance may be found. The questions need not be asked one after the other, in the order here given. They may be interspersed among the other tests. But, with this exception, the author desires to say that the order

[1] The material for the tests taken from the Healy scheme can be obtained from the C. H. Stoelting Company, Carroll Avenue, Chicago, U.S.A.

[2] See Appendix III.

## 44 THE PSYCHOLOGY OF THE CRIMINAL

in which his tests are given is not a matter of unimportance. The tests have been arranged in the order in which they are here described after long experimentation. Any worker who may think fit to give this particular scheme a trial, will do well, at least at first, to give the tests in the order here described.

(*a*) Name of the King. Generally known. (*b*) How long has he been King ? Generally known within a year or so. (*c*) Who was King before him ? Fairly generally known. (*d*) If Edward VII is correctly given in the previous answer ; Who came before King Edward ? This is seldom known. Of course it is twenty years since Queen Victoria's death, and many of the subjects were unborn, or small children, at that time. (*e*) Who is the Prince of Wales ? It is generally known that the Prince is the King's son, but only about half bring out the point that he is the eldest son. (*f*) Who is Prime Minister now ? So seldom known that the author has almost given up asking it. (*g*) What is a Prime Minister ? Practically never known, so given up. (*h*) When did the war begin ? Year almost always given correctly, and usually the month also. (*i*) What was the war about, how did it start, why did we go to war ? It is uncommon to get even a fairly intelligent answer. It seems to be a matter which the majority of subjects have never even considered. If pressed, most seem to have the idea that there was some personal quarrel between the King and the Kaiser. (*j*) Who were we fighting against ? Always known so far as Germany is concerned : the German menace appears to have been clearly understood. The allies of Germany are seldom known. (*k*) Who were our allies, who were fighting on our side ? France and Belgium usually given, the Australians often given, America hardly ever named. (*l*) What kind of ruler do they have in America, is he a king, or what do they call him ? That he is called a president is fairly often known, name very rarely

# THE OFFENDER'S CONSCIOUS MIND 45

known, even when Mr. Wilson was a very prominent figure. (m) What is the difference between a king and a president? Practically never known. This is one of Terman's tests for fourteen years of age. (n) What kind of chief ruler do they have in France? Practically never known. (o) Which is the bigger, Birmingham or London? Nearly always answered correctly. (p) How long would it take to go by train from Birmingham to London? Approximate time usually known. (p) Name some other large towns in England. The answers seldom go further than the Black Country towns, except that sea-side resorts such as Blackpool are often given. (q) Where are Paris, Berlin, Brussels, New York? Correct answers to all these given in about half the cases. (r) Names of the months in the year. Practically always correct, but many subjects are unable to give them other than by rote; e.g. they often fail if asked what month comes before October. This is a Terman test for nine years of age. (s) Who were Nelson, Wellington, Joseph Chamberlain? Very vague replies, surprisingly so in the third instance. (s) Number of different kinds of people seen in the streets in uniform. About nine are usually given, seldom more. It is not fair to ask this question of a case which comes from a country village. (t) How does a thermometer work? This is introduced because a thermometer is one of the pictures shown in the Heilbronner test. All know that it is used to tell the heat of a room, nearly all know that heat causes the mercury to rise, very few indeed can explain why heat has this effect. (u) Names of prominent football teams and their recent performances (boys and men). Nearly all take much interest. (v) Similar questions as to cricket. Very little interest shown. (w) Books read. The answers are humiliating to English literature. Many of the subjects appear never to have read a book since their school days. Some few get books from the public libraries. Authors' names are seldom

## 46 THE PSYCHOLOGY OF THE CRIMINAL

known, though the girls sometimes mention Mrs. Henry Wood. (*y*) Moving Picture Shows. Intense interest always shown. Not to care for the " pictures " is a most unusual phenomenon. Most of the subjects appear to prefer what are known as " serials " (wonderful productions in about fifteen weekly " parts "). Next to these, preference is shown for love dramas. The " comics " do not seem to be very popular . (*z*) Do you, or your father, belong to a Union ? If the answer is " yes "; then, What is a Union ? The answers are, as a rule, very vague, not often more than, " They settle about strikes ". (*aa*) Prices of such things as clothes and boots (and for girls the prices of food). These are usually given correctly. (*bb*) For girls, Can you cook ? Usual answer, " I can cook a bit ". (*cc*) For girls Can you make, or have you ever made, any of your own clothes ? Usual answer, " No ". (*dd*) What would you like to be if you could have the choice ? There is a great variety in the answers. But a very large percentage of the younger subjects seem to have no ideas on the matter, and no ambition whatever.

The paucity of information and the limited interests displayed is often quite amazing. And an examiner is sometimes inclined to wonder if our fifty years of universal education has been of much practical value. But to take too pessimistic a view would be unwarranted, until we have had tests made on similar lines amongst classes other than delinquents.

Such is the author's standard method. And he claims, and the results have confirmed the claim, that very valuable information can be obtained by this method. We have pointed out that various characteristics, e.g. memory, attention, observation, power of planning a task, ability to profit by errors, capacity to understand directions, and to grasp the essentials of a situation are all brought out. And we can form a definite opinion as to intelligence, and a judgment as to the existence of

# THE OFFENDER'S CONSCIOUS MIND    47

mental defect, so far as intelligence is concerned. " Normal " subjects usually do all, or the great majority, of the performance tests here described. Consequently, a failure in any considerable number of these tests is proof of defect of intelligence, especially as particular care is taken to score the results on the tests as generously as possible.

The author does not give, nor does he consider, any definite proportion of failures as being essential for the diagnosis of defect of intelligence. He admits the attraction of a fixed standard, such as we have in certain interpretations of the Binet scale. To be able to state a person's intelligence in terms of " mental age " is very seductive. But there are serious objections. There is the question of scoring. The Terman tests are all arranged so that they can be scored as success, half-success, or failure. But, in order to do this, we have to make use of a number of quite arbitrary conventions. The set of tests here described do not all lend themselves to such a system of scoring. Again, if a subject passed all the Terman tests for nine years of age, and failed in all the higher age tests, we might be entitled to say (apart from other considerations) that his " mental age " was nine years. But this result is seldom found. And to bring in the tests which he passes in higher years is only done by means of still more arbitrary conventions. It is not clear that we are entitled to talk of " mental age " as if it represented an actual reality. For to do this it is necessary to compare abnormal maturity with healthy immaturity. The propriety of saying that a man of fifty has the mental age of a child of eight years seems very doubtful. In this connexion it may be of interest to record what practically happens here. When the author has decided that a young subject is a mental defective, and that he should be certified under the Act, it very generally occurs that the case is separately examined by a colleague who uses the Terman scale.

## 48 THE PSYCHOLOGY OF THE CRIMINAL

The estimation of the subject's mentality by the two examinations, so far as the diagnosis of mental defect is concerned, has hardly differed in a single instance. It is claimed, however, that this set of tests is of more general applicability, and that much valuable information can be elicited by these tests which is not obtained so well by the Terman scale, if obtained at all.

The author is well aware that he is open to the charge of making a diagnosis of defect of intelligence depend upon the " general impression " formed by the examiner. But we do not require the presence of some fixed number of signs and symptoms before making a diagnosis of some " physical " ailment. Many such signs and symptoms can be enumerated as being often, or sometimes, present in pneumonia, let us say. But a physician would regard it as an unreasonable proposition that he must have some definite and fixed standard for his diagnosis. The situation is that, an examiner having been chosen, he must be trusted. He may rightly be required to prove his competence, but, this having been done, his opinion must be accepted. It is true that under certain circumstances he may be asked to give the reasons for his opinion. But the author thinks that the records of the results obtained on this scheme of tests supplies sufficient reasons. He realizes the importance of the decision. He recognizes the serious results which may accrue to the patient if the diagnosis of mental defect is formed, and the consequent need for much care in making this diagnosis. But he is prepared to accept the responsibility.

Even the most devoted adherent of the Binet scale will hardly claim that the non-attainment of any particular mental age is, *per se*, enough to establish mental deficiency as a diagnosis. The history of the case, and other points, must be weighed. No " Scale of Intelligence ", Binet or other, will ever give us a true estimation of an individual's status. There must

## THE OFFENDER'S CONSCIOUS MIND  49

be a thorough study, mental and physical, of the subject. And this mental study must include consideration of the effects of his history and environment.

We may have : (1) Cases of obvious mental defect, in which we want the confirmatory evidence of test results. (2) Cases in which the mental state is doubtful until an examination has been made. (3) Cases in which no idea of mental defect, in the sense of possible certification, arises, but in which we may want to form a general opinion as to a patient's mentality, and to discover the presence of any special ability or defect, in order that we may advise as to suitable treatment or disposal for the case.

Having established defect of intelligence from the point of view of possible certification under the Mental Deficiency Act, we may desire to confirm our view by the use of other tests. There is a great variety to choose from. And we may mention :—

1. *The Missing Features Test.* There is the Binet set, placed in the six-year group by Terman, although in the original scale it was included among the eight-year tests. Or, if something more elaborate is desired, there are other sets. Among these latter we may mention an excellent set used by the American Army authorities, whose great courtesy in providing him with a complete set of their material and their confidential directions, even before these had been published in America, the author wishes to take this opportunity of publicly acknowledging.

2. *Æsthetic Comparison* (Binet), e.g. differentiating between " pretty " and " ugly " faces.

3. *Naming colours* (Binet).

4. *Naming the months of the year.*

5. *Simple problems with coins and stamps.*

Or again, we may wish to proceed further in the other, the higher direction. There is here, also, a great variety of tests from which we may make choice. The

# 50 THE PSYCHOLOGY OF THE CRIMINAL

author has found the following likely to give valuable information.

1. *The Code Test.* This was originally devised by Healy. It is fully described by Terman, who places it in his sixteen-year, or " average-adult ", group. It is simply a form of " secret writing ". And it consists, essentially, in learning a series of 26 systematically related associations, in the form of signs, each of which corresponds to a letter of the alphabet. Intelligent boys take much interest in the test. It does not seem so attractive to girls.

2. Fernald[1] has a useful " *Ethical Discrimination* " *Test*, which consists in arranging in the order of their gravity a series of 10 offences. It is, of course, a test of intelligence, using the offences as integers.

3. *Ethical Perception.* This test is described by Healy. As used by him it consists in gauging the subject's power of appreciating and giving a reasoned solution of two ethical problems. For various causes the present author does not make use of one of these. But the other problem is excellent, and runs as follows :
" A settlement was once besieged by a large body of Indians because the Chief thought that one of the white men had done him an injury, though he really had not done so. The Chief sent word to the captain of the village that if the man was given up to him he would go away, but, if not, he would burn the village and kill the people. The captain and the people knew that if the Indians attacked them they would be very likely to capture the village, and, at least, would kill a good many of the people. They also knew that their fellow villager was innocent, and that to give him up meant torture and death for him. What was the right thing for the captain of the village to do, and why ? What would you have done if you had been captain ? " The problem may be read to the subject, or it may be

[1] " American Journal of Insanity ", Vol. XLVIII.

## THE OFFENDER'S CONSCIOUS MIND 51

printed on a card and given him to read. He is then asked for his answer. It is not so much the " rightness " or " wrongness " of the solution that has to be considered; there are the reasons which the subject gives as well. And there is the way in which he gives his solution. Some present it in a doubtful and hesitating manner, and at the least suggestion of opposition on the part of the examiner will entirely alter their answer. Giving this problem as the subject for a short essay with a class of intelligent boys and girls can be recommended, but this does not bring out the characteristic last mentioned. It is interesting to get answers from young subjects who have seen military service. They sometimes try to cover complete ignorance of the real issues involved by a great display of military knowledge on details of fortification.

And there are a number of other excellent tests among which we may mention the mazes, in which the subject is given the plan of a maze of more or less complexity, and is required with a pencil to trace the best path to the exit. We have the " analogy " test. The subject is presented with a series of problems of this kind: Dog : puppy = cat : tiger horse kitten cow, and has to underline that one of the last four words which best completes the analogy. There is a test of " common sense ", in which the subject is given a series of questions which are each provided with three answers, of which only one is reasonable; and has to indicate the answer which he prefers. There are some good graduated tests in " reasoning " by Cyril Burt.[1] And there is the test in which the subject is required to supply the opposites to a list of common adjectives.

So far we have considered tests as applied to individuals, because our particular work is, and must be, a personal and individual matter. But there are some splendid sets of " group " tests, of which the Terman

[1] " Journal of Experimental Pedagogy ", 1919.

## 52 THE PSYCHOLOGY OF THE CRIMINAL

and the Otis may be mentioned. There is a great opening for the use of tests of this kind. If this work were done we should have a much better guide than we possess at present to the degree of intelligence which may reasonably be expected from various classes of people. And, if we knew this, we should then have some standard with which to compare our delinquents. At present we have no such standard. If we compare them with the range of tests known on the Terman scale as " average adult ", we should find that the great majority would fail. This would only be negative evidence. And to test them on the lower ages would give unreliable results, for the reasons set out earlier in this book. These considerations, among others, led to the elaboration of the scheme of tests just described. One decided defect of the various forms of group tests is that, being given by means of questions which are to be answered on paper, the personal judgment of the examiner is quite eliminated. This is unfortunate, because much can be learned from the careful observation by the examiner of the subject's attitude to the tests and the manner in which he approaches them.

It is objected that all these tests only measure one factor in a case, that of intelligence, and that there are other factors to be considered. This objection must be duly weighed. And in this connexion there is most interesting evidence from America.

On their entry into the Great War, the U.S. Army authorities decided to have a psychological examination made of all their drafted men. This, the first examination of this kind made on a large scale, was applied to about two million recruits. The tests used will be found fully described in the book by Yoakum and Yerkes.[1] The men were graded, on the results of this examination, in various classes. Men who failed to reach a certain standard were put back for individual

[1] " Mental Tests in the American Army."

## THE OFFENDER'S CONSCIOUS MIND 53

examination, and if found unlikely to become useful in the army were discharged. We need not point out how much trouble would have been saved had such a plan been adopted in this country from the start. But the important point from our present aspect is this: It was recognized from the first that intelligence is not the only thing required to make a useful soldier. And so the men were also graded by their immediate military commanders on the results of the men's performances at their ordinary military duties, and quite apart from the psychological examination. It was found that the two gradings only differed in less than one-half of one per cent of all the cases. It was also found that only men who attained a fairly high mental rating could be usefully trained as officers or non-commissioned officers. And further, and this fact is most important, it was discovered that the " disciplinary " units, to which ill-conducted men were assigned, contained a far higher proportion of men of a low grade of intelligence than did the ordinary units. As the result of the selection of men which was thus made possible, the ratio of crimes in the American army was far less than had been anticipated as the result of experience in former wars.

The American Army authorities point out that the rating which a man earns on their mental tests " furnishes a fairly reliable index of his ability to learn, to think quickly and accurately, to analyse a situation, to maintain a state of mental alertness, and to comprehend and follow instructions. The score is little affected by schooling: some of the highest records have been made by men who had not completed the eighth grade."[1]

They further point out that " the mental tests are not intended to replace other methods of judging a man's value to the service. It would be a mistake to assume that they tell us infallibly what kind of

[1] " Army Mental Tests ", Washington, D.C., 1918.

## 54 THE PSYCHOLOGY OF THE CRIMINAL

soldier a man will make. They merely help us to do this by measuring one important element in a soldier's equipment, namely, intelligence. They do not measure loyalty, bravery, power to command, or the emotional traits which make a man " carry on ". However, in the long run, these qualities are more likely to be found in men of superior intelligence than in men who are intellectually inferior. Intelligence is perhaps the most important single factor in soldier efficiency, apart from physical health." And, although there are exceptions, as a rule physical health and intelligence go together.

Nor is this the only piece of evidence of the kind. The Otis scheme of tests has been used with the employées of a number of large business establishments in America. And the results obtained from this testing corresponded, in the vast majority of cases, with the estimation of the employées formed by those who were connected with them in their ordinary daily work. Solomon anticipated these results many centuries ago. Have we not been rather inclined to forget the lessons he tried to teach ?

After all, what is intelligence ? It must mean a combination of a number of distinct mental character- istics. Otis says that we have to consider intelligence, personal qualities, and professional value. (He is speaking of business employées, but his remarks have only to be slightly altered for application to other classes.) He finds that there is a marked correlation between intelligence and the two other qualifications. He defines intelligence as " a combination of resourceful- ness, ingenuity, ease of learning, and ability to under- stand directions easily, and to arrive at a sensible decision in a new and problematical situation ". Personal qualities he defines as " neatness, taste, agreeableness of personality, initiative, loyalty, relia- bility, and co-operation " Professional value he defines as " covering training and experience both in and

## THE OFFENDER'S CONSCIOUS MIND 55

previous to the present occupation". He says that "anyone who makes a high score on his system is surely intelligent, and that is impossible for a really dull person to make a high score, but that confusion from extreme nervousness [this factor is, in itself, worthy of note] or other cause may sometimes prevent a subject from making the score which he should do". With these remarks the present author is in complete agreement. It is very necessary to be as certain as possible that a subject is in a proper condition for testing. Illness may make a great difference in the results obtained. And the same may be said of nervousness. Hence arises one advantage in having the subject in some institution while his case is being investigated. He can then be given time to become habituated to his surroundings, and to overcome any nervousness. And he gets accustomed to the medical examiner. A suitable time can then be fixed for formal examination with the tests. It is also well that the examiner should be in a suitable mood for conducting the examination. Above all things, the examination must not be hurried.

The exhibition of a scheme of tests often appears to change materially the attitude of the subject towards the examiner. Sullenness and resistance may have existed before, but the author has seen these disappear completely when the tests have been tactfully presented. It seems as though this examination causes the subject to realize, as nothing else does, that the object of the examination is to help him as far as possible.

The possible effect of coaching on the test results must be considered. So far as the present scheme of tests is concerned, and in Court work, this may be neglected. But with the well-known schemes, such as the Binet, the chance of coaching has to be remembered And if any scheme, such as the Otis, became in general use for Civil Service or similar examinations, precautions

## 56 THE PSYCHOLOGY OF THE CRIMINAL

would have to be taken to discount the effects of coaching. It would be possible for a tutor to cause a comparatively unintelligent candidate to attain a higher grade than he deserved. The effect of practice in some of the tests, such as the analogies, might be very marked. The Binet scheme is so much used that it is not uncommon to get hints, confirmed on inquiry, that certain of the tests have been previously given to the subject and remembered by him. The author has, however, had the opportunity in a few cases of giving his scheme of tests to the same subject with a year's interval. The result has been almost identically the same on each occasion. Mistakes are made in the same tests, and in the same way. Suggestibility, as shown by the tests, has been indicated in the same way each time.

The objection is sometimes taken that the results obtained on tests vary with the social position, previous environment, and educational facilities of the subject. In purely educational tests the latter facilities must be carefully considered, and, in the case of an older subject, how far he has followed up these advantages in later life. And the value of tests of general information and interests must be weighed in the light of the subject's environment. Binet himself pointed out that children from wealthier homes did grade somewhat higher than those from poorer surroundings. This would make more difference in his scheme of tests than in the author's, on account of the fact that the Binet scheme is very favourable to subjects with good language ability. Terman well points out that his tests were not intended for deaf-mutes, or for those who had passed their lives in a cage, but for those who had the opportunities of making the ordinary social contacts.

Haggerty of the University of Minnesota, says that intelligence tests are not intended to be substitutes for

# THE OFFENDER'S CONSCIOUS MIND 57

ordinary common sense on the part of the examiner. He says: " When a physician reads a thermometer, counts the pulse, and measures blood-pressure, he does not throw away his powers of personal judgment. He interprets these data in terms of all the other things which he knows about the patient and about human nature in general. So the examiner must use the results of his tests to supplement, correct, or reinforce his ordinary powers of observation." All this is well worth remembering in view of the somewhat extravagant claims which appear to be made in some quarters about the value of the Binet tests.

Quite apart from the answers given to questions and the results obtained from other tests, the subject's general demeanour and bearing should be observed. Is he bright and cheerful ? What is his attitude towards the examiner ? And opportunity should be taken to gather what the view of the subject is as to the particular orm of delinquency with which he may happen to be charged, and towards delinquency in general. We shall have more to say, later, on the matter of the anti-social attitude.

Valuable information may often be obtained from the attendants if the subject is in an institution. This is one advantage of having the subject under observation in some form of remand institution where the attendants are, as they should be, persons skilled in making observations and with tact in managing inmates. Note should be taken of the subject's conduct in the ward. Is he good-tempered, or quarrelsome, with other inmates ? Is he willing and desirous to assist by doing small jobs of work in the ward ? Does he make use of the books and games provided ? Does he show interest in his surroundings ? And other points will suggest themselves.

It need hardly be said that every opportunity should be taken to get all possible information as to the subject's

## 58 THE PSYCHOLOGY OF THE CRIMINAL

former history, work, companions, etc.; also of his family-history, in the broadest sense.

A few of the more common difficulties met with in this branch of mental investigation must be briefly considered.

(a) On the examiner's side there may be fatigue. This can only be guarded against by taking care, if possible, not to attempt mental testing when tired. Or he may not feel " in the mood " for testing, as we say. In so far as this is not laziness, it is difficult to guard against. No one who has not tried it can have any idea how tiring and trying the continual examination of delinquents may become. Even the repetition of the same tests time after time, and seeing the same errors constantly repeated, is very apt to give rise to a feeling of irritation, which has to be sternly controlled. All teachers will appreciate this point. Only intense interest in the work, and full evaluation of its importance will suffice to keep the examiner at it. And he can only strive to keep his mind fresh for his task, and endeavour to be as free from distractions as possible. Both these desiderata are, unhappily, hard of attainment.

(b) There may be faults in the environment. These conditions are more under our control. The room used for examination should be well lighted, and in winter it is absolutely necessary that it should be comfortably warmed. It is best to have the subject seated opposite to the examiner, at a table on which there is ample room for the manipulation of the various tests. Only the very briefest notes should be made at the time, and this should be done as unostentatiously as possible. A system of shorthand is soon adopted which can be elaborated immediately the examination is over. It is most disturbing to the subject to get the idea that his words are being taken down verbatim. Male subjects are seen alone, in a room with a glass-covered window

## THE OFFENDER'S CONSCIOUS MIND 59

on the other side of which there is an attendant, who does not, however, stare ostentatiously at the subject. With female subjects the author most strictly insists on the presence of a female attendant in the room. The attendant can occupy herself in reading or knitting, and experience has shown that her presence does not affect the value of the examination.

(c) There may be disturbing conditions on the part of the subject.

(1) Shyness from unfamiliar surroundings. This is best obviated by allowing time to elapse before the final testing is done. To spring a set of tests suddenly upon a new subject is only to court failure. The Birmingham prison cases are always remanded for a week, and this period is extended if desired. The first four or five days are allowed to pass by with only simple general conversation with the subject, unless an attempt is to be made to see if analysis is likely to prove useful. The examiner must try to win the subject's confidence and to demonstrate that the sole desire of all the officials is to be as helpful as possible. Much is to be learned by quiet talks with the subject, and by the observations which can be made by experienced, sympathetic, and tactful attendants. The quiet routine of the remand department in the Hospital, with its attractive literature, pleasant surroundings, and simple games, soon produces its effect, and makes the subject realize that all possible endeavours are being made to understand and to help him. We have found, at Birmingham, that simple fancy needlework is of great value with female patients. Then, towards the close of the remand period, a suitable time for the formal examination can be selected, the case can be fully considered, and the report made. All these advantages are only to be had in an institution. During the examination, praise for his test performances (even when these are poor) should be freely given to the subject.

# 60 THE PSYCHOLOGY OF THE CRIMINAL

(2) There may be emotional disturbance produced by arrest and conveyance to the prison. And this fact should put us on our guard against forming too hasty an opinion. But, so long as there is no *conviction*, this emotional disturbance soon passes off. The subject seems to be at his best when he realizes that his case is being carefully considered, when he feels himself to be a problem which the examiner is trying to solve. It is quite otherwise after conviction : the emotional disturbance produced by this, and the anti-social feeling which may thus be engendered, always make examinations immediately after conviction to be quite unreliable, and in some cases may make all examinations during sentence useless. We shall have occasion to touch on this anti-social feeling later.

(3) Fatigue. This can hardly occur if the precautions just indicated are observed.

(4) The possible presence of marked physical defects, such as defective vision, or deafness, must be allowed for. So careful physical examination must always be a preliminary procedure.

(5) There may be complete refusal to attempt any tests, or there may be deliberate deception. These conditions are very rare. But when they do occur they indicate mental characteristics which are, in themselves, of much importance. Laziness may also be seen, and this has its import. Lack of attention and of perseverance are also to be noted.

(6) There are certain peculiar mental conditions met with in epilepsy and in hysteria, which we shall deal with in Chapter **V**. These often produce very irregular and puzzling results with any scheme of mental tests.

We cannot close this chapter without giving some short consideration to two phrases which are often used as expressing certain characteristics in delinquents and others.

1. " *Will Power.*" In so far as this implies the

# THE OFFENDER'S CONSCIOUS MIND  61

existence of an entity called the " will ", in the sense indicated in Chapter I, we must altogether reject it. We cannot speak, scientifically, of a person having a " weak " or a " strong " will. Argument on this subject of the " will " would be out of place, and, indeed, is quite useless. Either a man accepts the deterministic position, or he does not. And this book is, throughout, written on a deterministic basis.

But the term " will power " is frequently used. And it certainly seems to describe some more or less definite entity. The shortest consideration shows that the phrase has a number of different connotations. And two of these must be mentioned.

(a) The expression " weakness of will power " may mean undue susceptibility to the influence of suggestion. This means the readiness to accept suggestions arising from sources without the mind. It is limited by a disinclination to accept suggestions from sources which the mind considers to be hostile, as well as those which would be in conflict with some strong complex which is already in the mind. And it is increased in the case of suggestions made by sources which the mind regards as having authority, and also in the case of those suggestions which are in agreement with complexes already present in the mind. (On the subject of " complexes " see the next chapter.) Knowledge of the susceptibility of many persons to the influence of suggestion is made constant use of by advertisers and the like. Susceptibility to suggestion differs greatly in degree in different persons. And in the case of a man who is highly suggestible we may suppose that the forces which impel him to some action, and the forces which inhibit such action, are very evenly balanced. This explains why alcohol weakens the will. It tends to paralyse the inhibiting forces. The expression " strong will " may mean the exact opposite to the above condition. Or it may mean a tendency to what

## 62 THE PSYCHOLOGY OF THE CRIMINAL

is termed " contra-suggestion ". Suggestion is taken by some (e.g. Tansley) as a non-rational process. In a sense this may be true. But, ultimately, the process is under the guidance of the intellect, for, as a rule, mental defectives tend to be highly suggestible.

(b) " Weakness of will " may mean lack of perseverance and attention. Of course the lack of these characteristics is, in a sense, an example of " self-suggestion ". The unconscious mind makes the suggestion that laziness is preferable to work, that an easy course of action is more to be desired than a more difficult course.

Stephen[1] puts the matter thus : " By the assertion that a man has a strong will, I mean that he distinctly knows what he permanently wants and means to do ; that his motives and intentions do not change from day to day, and are not immediately altered by the discovery of difficulties in the way of their performance." And he goes on to say that this view implies that will depends upon intellect. This is, in effect, what Spinoza taught when he says : " Intellect and will are one and the same ".[2]

2. We have also the question of *Emotional Control*. There is no doubt that the power of control of the emotions is diminished in many delinquents, and especially so in those who are mentally defective or subnormal. Ultimately this resolves itself into a matter of the intelligence. An infant's power of emotional control is, originally, nil. But we gradually learn that we have to control our emotional expression in accordance with the commands of the particular part of society in which we live. The degree of control which is expected varies within wide limits in any particular society. But, on the whole, the higher is the degree

[1] op. cit.
[2] " Ethics ", Part II, Corollary to Prop. XLIX, and the Scolium following.

## THE OFFENDER'S CONSCIOUS MIND 63

of intelligence, the greater is the power of emotional control.

Absence of emotional display, apparently due to a real absence of emotion, is a symptom of certain forms of insanity.

For a general discussion of the results obtained from this scheme of tests, see a paper entitled " Mental Tests for Delinquents," by the author and Dr. G. W. Pailthorpe, published in the " Lancet," 1923, vol. II, pp. 112, ff.

### CHAPTER III

## THE INVESTIGATION OF THE OFFENDER'S UNCONSCIOUS MIND

IN our last chapter we dealt with the investigation of the offender's conscious mind. Much excellent work has been, and is still being, done in this direction. Much still remains to be done, for the ground has, as yet, hardly been scratched over. The author would not wish to detract, even in the least degree, from the value of the information which is thus obtainable. But we now have to enter upon the consideration of an even more important matter, the investigation of the offender's *unconscious* mind.

The subject of this and the following chapter is the relation of this investigation to our study of offenders. But this study of the unconscious mind is comparatively new and of vast extent. Knowledge of the methods used in the study, and of the results thus obtainable, is not very far advanced even among medical practitioners. This book is intended for all who are interested in the study of offenders, and is not addressed to a purely medical audience ; so some description of the theory of the unconscious mind, and of the methods used in its exploration, is a necessary preliminary.

There have been hints of the importance of the unconscious mind for many years, but these have been, for the most part, vague and unconvincing. Just so, the movements of the planet Uranus perplexed astronomers for many years, until Adams and Leverrier solved

## THE OFFENDER'S UNCONSCIOUS MIND 65

the problem by discovering the existence and the influence of Neptune.

Discoverers of scientific truths have never been wholly lacking in any age, and each is entitled to his due place in the temple of fame. But from time to time human thought is enriched by the promulgation of an hypothesis, based upon scientific research, which revolutionizes all previous ideas, and which gives us not so much information concerning an hitherto unknown fact, as an entirely new orientation of our knowledge. Copernicus and Darwin are, perhaps, the most eminent instances of such discoverers. Each changed our whole conception of our origin and destiny. But there has arisen another in this, our time. Sigmund Freud, by his hypothesis of the unconscious, has radically altered all our views of human nature.

Freud's discovery was originally made in the course of his researches into the nature of hysteria, and its original application was in the therapeutic cure of that neurosis. It has since become a method of scientific investigation. And this, as well as the former application, rests upon a body of doctrine. Modifications of Freud's views have been promulgated by others. And these modifications appear, in the author's opinion, to rest upon a fundamental and irreconcilable difference from the views of Freud. The subject is, at present, highly controversial. And the controversy is being waged with much heat, and in the midst of much dust. It may, perhaps, be as well to state, at the outset, that this book is written, so far as the subject of psychoanalysis is concerned, from the Freudian position.

Like his two great predecessors just mentioned, Freud has been, and still is, the object of contumely and abuse. This is, in part, due to the fact that his discovery is, as yet, little understood. But it is also due, in part, to the fact that the bearings of his discovery are only too well understood. Many of our most cherished illusions

# 66 THE PSYCHOLOGY OF THE CRIMINAL

will have to be discarded when the full glory of his work is seen. The effect of his discovery, in one particular direction, will be appreciated when we come to consider the application of his theory to Court work, and to point out how profoundly it modifies our estimation of offenders, and how it should alter our dealings with them.

In the mind of every individual there are modes of thought and instinctive tendencies which are derived by means of inheritance from past ages. Recognition of the existence of these, and of their importance, is a matter of absolute necessity. It is not possible for us to understand any organism unless we are acquainted with its biological history, and this, of course, applies to the human mind. McDougall defines instincts as " certain innate specific tendencies which are common to all members of any one species ".[1] And he further says, " The instinctive impulses determine the ends of all activities, and supply the driving power by which all mental activities are sustained ".

The great primary instincts each have certain emotions closely connected with them. These instincts and emotions have been enumerated and classified in various ways by different authors. McDougall's account of them is, perhaps, the best.[2]

These primitive instincts are, as we have said, the mainsprings of all mental life. An instinct may be regarded as the expression of an emotion which arises in response to a group of sensations. And all the instincts may be grouped under four, or perhaps three, main heads. We have the instinct of self-nutrition, the instinct of self-preservation (probably the first of these two instincts may be regarded as part of the second), the sex instinct, and the herd instinct which impels man to act as a member of some larger or smaller group or society. The relative importance of these

[1] " Social Psychology."     [2] ibid.

# THE OFFENDER'S UNCONSCIOUS MIND 67

main instincts is a question which has given rise to much acrimonious controversy. To the author there seems to be no doubt as to the supreme importance of the sex instinct. There is its complexity, the large part which it has been shown to play in the production of the neuroses, the constant conflict between it and the herd instinct, and the fact that the primary object of every living organism is the perpetuation of its species. Regarded from the animal standpoint, and this is how the unconscious may, in a sense, be said to " regard " the matter, the whole aim of man's existence is the perpetuation of the species. Foster's words, written over thirty years ago, may be quoted in this connexion : " When the animal kingdom is surveyed from a broad standpoint it becomes obvious that the ovum, or its correlative, the spermatozoon, is the goal of an individual existence ; that life is a cycle, beginning in an ovum, and coming round to an ovum again. The greater part of the actions which, looking from a near point of view at the higher animals alone, we are apt to consider as eminently the purposes for which animals come into existence, when viewed from the distant outlook whence the whole living world is surveyed, fade away into the likeness of the mere by-play of ovum-bearing organisms. The animal body is in reality a vehicle for ova ; and after the life of the parent has become potentially renewed in the offspring, the body remains as a cast-off envelope whose future is but to die."[1]

Some of these considerations as to the importance of the sex instinct will have to be taken up more fully later on. But we are, fortunately, not required to enter into the controversy just mentioned. The acceptance of any particular view on this point does not seem essential to the theory of psycho-analysis. It suffices that we should recognize what few will deny, the importance of the sex instinct. These primary instincts

[1] " Text Book of Physiology ", 1891, Vol. IV.

# 68 THE PSYCHOLOGY OF THE CRIMINAL

lie in the unconscious mind, and the energy produced by them is constantly welling up from the unconscious into consciousness.

Freud uses the term " conscious " for all mental processes of which a person is aware at any given moment, whether distinctly or indistinctly. Closely connected with the conscious, and not sharply demarcated from it, is what he terms the " foreconscious ", or the " preconscious ", which contains the memories of which a person is not at any particular moment aware, but which can be recalled into consciousness without special difficulty.

It may be well to remark here that when we speak of " areas " or " places " in the mind, and of " barriers " or " obstacles " in the way of mental processes, we are only using figurative expressions. We are obliged to translate our ideas into intelligible language. The theories of the " newer " psychology are, after all, only hypotheses; and they are accepted by many of those who have studied them, because they appear to fit the facts better than do other hypotheses.

The unconscious forms the basis of the entire mind. It has been termed the " primary " unconscious, in order to distinguish it from the " secondary " or " Freudian " unconscious, to which we shall refer shortly, the contents of which are formed in a very different manner. The great primary instincts, and the elements of the mind which are connected with them, lie originally in this primary unconscious. And from the unconscious continually passes the psychic energy which gives activity to the mental elements in the foreconscious. The contents of the primary unconscious are very vague. Except in the form of vague emotion they attain access to the conscious by taking on forms which belong to the foreconscious.

We are now in a position to grasp the meaning of the term " complex ", of which we shall hear much. Bernard

## THE OFFENDER'S UNCONSCIOUS MIND 69

Hart defines a complex as " a system of connected ideas with a strong emotional tone, and a tendency to produce actions of a certain definite character ".[1] It is in this sense that the present author intends to use the word, whether the system of ideas is situated in the unconscious or in the conscious. Some writers confine the term complex to a system of ideas which was at one time present to consciousness, but which has been relegated to the unconscious by a process which is known as " repression ", and of which we shall have more to say directly. These writers use the term " constellation " for such a system of ideas when it exists in the conscious mind or in the foreconscious. But this differentiation of terms seems to the author to be unfortunate as tending to obscure one of Freud's great basic principles, namely, the unity of all mental life. As Freud himself puts it: " The unconscious is the larger circle which includes within itself the smaller circle of the conscious; everything conscious has its preliminary step in the unconscious. . . . The unconscious is the real psychic; its inner nature is just as unknown to us as the reality of the external world, and it is just as imperfectly reported to us through the data of consciousness as is the external world through the indications of our sensory organs."[2]

Examples of complexes are quite familiar to each one of us. And many complexes are quite conscious. The greater part of the energy which we apply to the service of our daily life, our professional and other interests, and our amusements, is the result of the action of these complexes which are in harmony with the mind as a whole. But a complex may be out of harmony with the mind as a whole. And, if this is the case, a conflict will result between the mind and the offending complex;

[1] " The Psychology of Insanity ".
[2] " The Interpretation of Dreams ", English Translation, p. 562.

## 70 THE PSYCHOLOGY OF THE CRIMINAL

or there may be a condition of conflict between individual complexes. A condition of acute conflict usually does not, and perhaps cannot, last long. And three results may follow:

1. We may have separation of a complex from the mind as a whole. Instances of this are not far to seek. We all know the man who keeps his religion and his business in " water-tight compartments ", as we say. And this is no doubt what also happens in the cases in which some offender, e.g. a burglar, carries on a respectable family life.

2. We may have a condition of chronic conflict between two complexes, or between a complex and the mind as a whole. And each may gain the victory from time to time.

3. A complex may become repressed into the unconscious. The unconscious into which this repression takes place is regarded by Freud as being, in some respects, distinct from the primary unconscious of which we have already spoken. It has been termed the " secondary " or " Freudian " unconscious. This distinction appears to the author to be unfortunate. For it tends to convey the idea of separate areas in the unconscious. Whereas the distinction is not so much one of location as one of process. In the one case the mental elements are in the unconscious originally, never having been present to consciousness. In the other case the repressed elements have once been present in consciousness, and have been banished therefrom by an active process. (We may compare the one series of events to the German army striving to invade France, and the other series to the case of Germans who were originally in France, have been banished therefrom by the conflict of war, and who are ever striving to return, and perhaps succeeding in this attempt by disguising themselves.) The mind as a whole is the loser by this process of repression. More or less energy has to be

# THE OFFENDER'S UNCONSCIOUS MIND 71

employed in maintaining the repression of the banished complex. And the repressed complex, although it has been banished to the unconscious, is not dead. It is constantly acting. And various results may follow from this :—

(a) The energy attached to the emotions of the repressed complex may become what is termed " sublimated ", and so may be admitted into consciousness. It may be utilized for various purposes (social or other) which are in harmony with the mind as a whole, and are also in harmony with the ideals of the particular part of society to which the individual happens to belong. This process, again, is quite familiar. We all know instances of the man or woman in whose case the energy derived from the sex instinct has been " sublimated " into altruistic labours for others, the pursuit of sport, the care of animals, and the like.

(b) Unable to be sublimated, the psychic energy of the repressed complex may take on some disguised form, and so may produce actions the real cause of which the subject may be quite unaware of. There will often be a process of what is called " rationalization ", that is to say, the subject will produce what are to him most excellent reasons for acting as he does act, and may be most indignant if the true reason for his actions is pointed out to him. This is one of the chief difficulties in psycho-analysis, and is one cause of what are termed the " resistances " which have to be overcome in that process. Perhaps the thing which a man least desires to understand is himself, and the understanding of self is the object of psycho-analysis. To take some examples : no demonstration is needed to explain the original cause of those embraces of lovers which are tolerated by the conventions of society. Yet this origin is quite unrecognized by the great majority of women, and by some men. And the perpetrators of the embraces might be most highly indignant if the underlying motive

# 72 THE PSYCHOLOGY OF THE CRIMINAL

for their actions was pointed out to them. The politician, again, will assert, most emphatically, that all his labours are actuated by what he considers to be the good of society. They may actually be so actuated in some cases ; but, in others, the motive is clearly due to the instinct of self assertion, or even to still " lower " motives. Let the reader, if he is a keen politician, reflect a little on this. He will at once recognize the truth of these remarks as regards the leaders of the party opposed to that of his choice, whichever that party may be. Then let him consider the way in which a friend, who happens to espouse the opposite party, will regard the matter. We see, in Court work, all kinds of instances in which the psychic energy of a repressed complex may escape into consciousness in a disguised form.

(c) A repressed complex may regain its position in consciousness, replacing an antagonistic complex, which latter may, in its turn, become repressed. This alternating process of repression and escape may continue, much in the same way as that in which the man and the woman come out of their pent-houses in the old-fashioned weather apparatus. We then get what is known as an " alternating personality ". There are two main forms of this : (1) True dual personality, of which the case of " Dr. Jekyll " and " Mr. Hyde " is the most famous in literature, but of which there have been numerous illustrations in real life, vouched for in scientific works. Such dual personalities may be the explanation of certain criminal offences. As we proceed with our work at psycho-analysis it seems quite certain that we shall definitely establish this fact, and that our law-makers and administrators will be obliged to give it due consideration in dealing with offenders. (2) We may have what are known as " fugue states ". In these the subject is confused (" disorientated ") in time and in place, although the personality is regarded as

# THE OFFENDER'S UNCONSCIOUS MIND 73

remaining the same. Such states are far from uncommon, and their recognition explains many actions which would otherwise remain obscure. These states are common among epileptics, and may precede, replace, or follow the typical " fit ". There is a classical instance of an American preacher, who disappeared from his home, and was found two months later keeping a small shop 200 miles away. Extreme instances of dual personality are not very common, but minor instances are far from rare. In these latter attacks there is not, as a rule, complete loss of memory (" amnesia ") for the actions of the other personality. We have to recognize the existence of these cases of dual personality. But it must be admitted that difficulties will occur when Courts are called upon to deal with them. Some of these cases are certainly amenable to treatment. But treatment, in any adequate sense of the word, is incompatible with a definite sentence of legal punishment. We shall have some remarks to make on this head later in this book.

(d) A repressed complex may escape into consciousness by taking the form of a physical symptom. In this case we get what is known as a " neurosis " or a " psycho-neurosis ". This matter will be rendered more comprehensible if we take an example from the late war. A soldier at the front may have a conflict between two complexes. There will be the complex which results from the instinct of self-preservation, urging him to escape from a dangerous and appalling situation. In opposition to this is the complex resulting from the herd instinct, perhaps backed by the instinct of self-assertion, urging him to remain at his post of duty. The result of this conflict may be a victory for this second complex, and the first complex, that of self-preservation, is vanquished and repressed. But this repressed complex may make its escape into conscious ness in the form of some physical disability, e.g. a

# 74 THE PSYCHOLOGY OF THE CRIMINAL

paralysis of a limb, or an attack of blindness. This result has the effect of the formation of a compromise between the conscious desire to remain at his post and the unconscious desire to escape from danger. Under similar circumstances there is reason to think that the repressed complex may escape into consciousness in the form of a mental symptom. The whole subject of the formation of the neuroses is of vast importance in its connexion with delinquency, and especially so at the present time. But we must defer consideration of this for a moment, in order that the course of the present exposition may not be interrupted.

(e) A repressed complex may lead an autonomous life in the unconscious, and its energy may be displayed in symbolic form in order that its real meaning may not be appreciated by the conscious mind. There are different varieties of this process. Many religious observances are of this nature. The reader will be able to find instances if he reflects upon the observances of some religion other than his own. This idea of symbolism leads us to a consideration of what Freud terms the " censor " or the " censorship ". He adopts the hypothesis that there is a process which prevents primitive emotions and unacceptable repressed thoughts and memories from entering consciousness in their original shape. To evade the activity of this " censor ", the emotions, thoughts, and memories strive to get into consciousness by clothing themselves in symbolic shapes. When we come to consider dreams we shall have to deal with this subject more fully. The censor or censorship is really the sum-total of the existing inhibiting tendencies at any given time. It is perhaps unfortunate that Freud has made use of a term which might imply the existence of some personified function, such as the " will " of theologians, or the " conscience ". But no better term seems devisable, without undue circumlocution. And if the reader will keep in mind

## THE OFFENDER'S UNCONSCIOUS MIND 75

the fact that Freud's whole theory is but an hypothesis, he will have no difficulty in avoiding the confusion of names with things.

(f) A repressed complex may escape into consciousness and may dominate the whole of consciousness in the form of an attack of insanity (a " psychosis "). There are many instances of this. And the subject is of great interest. But, inasmuch as persons who are " certifiably insane " are soon removed from the purview of Courts, to pursue this point further would take us beyond our scope.

(g) It has been urged by some that a repressed complex may issue into consciousness in the form of what is termed a " moral symptom ". This implies the existence of a special " moral sense ". And, in Chapter I, we adopted the position that such a " moral sense " is non-existent, and also that there is no " absolute " morality. A complex may produce actions which are contrary to the commonly accepted, the conventional code of our age, nation, etc. This is, of course, quite usual. But it is better, in the author's opinion, to avoid the use of the words " moral " and " morality ".

Not long since a writer referred to the unconscious as a " lumber room ". This reveals a misapprehension. The importance of the contents of the unconscious lies not in their static but in their dynamic character. We have seen that the basis of the unconscious consists of the great primitive instincts. Psychic energy is constantly welling up from these And far more of our psychic life than was once supposed, and more than many persons are even now willing to recognize, results from the action of these instincts. Again, there are constant repressions into the unconscious. These repressed emotions are not simply stored away. Their repression is an active process, quite distinct from " passive " forgetting, and they are constantly striving to obtain outlet into consciousness. Conflict in the

## 76 THE PSYCHOLOGY OF THE CRIMINAL

conscious mind may produce repression. And, repression having been achieved, the repressed elements are retained in the unconscious by an active process.

Various similes have been employed to illustrate the unity of all mental life. Perhaps the best is that of islands—some greater, some smaller—arising from the ocean. They appear to be quite unconnected, and to be separate entities. But we know them to be connected through their bases and the ocean bed. The various parts of this ocean bed lie at very different depths beneath the surface of the water. Further, we realize that sea and land are one entity, the planet on which we live.

No realization of the theory of psycho-analysis is possible without grasping the doctrine of " psychical determinism." This doctrine states that our every action is determined by the circumstances which exist at the moment, together with the whole mass of former experiences, whether remembered or forgotten. Probably even the most " voluntary " act is more determined by unconscious motives than it is by conscious deliberation. Every action which we perform, without exception, as well as every precedent mental process, is the only one which could possibly occur under the particular circumstances. It need hardly be said that this doctrine is entirely opposed to the popular idea of what is known as " free-will ". Deterministic views have, of course, been held by some of the greatest minds in all ages. Volumes have been written on both sides of the question, and the author has no intention of entering into the debate. No better summary can be had than that by R. M. McConnell.[1] According to the doctrine of psychical determinism, there is no such thing as chance in the psychical world any more than there is chance in the physical world. An uncaused psychical phenomenon is as unthinkable a thing as is an uncaused physical

[1] " Criminal Responsibility."

# THE OFFENDER'S UNCONSCIOUS MIND 77

phenomenon. Every psychical phenomenon is caused, just as is every physical phenomemon, and both kinds of phenomena are always the only possible ones under the particular existing circumstances. The doctrine is unacceptable to many, and this for various reasons. The question has been much confused by the introduction of notions of predestination to some particular fate in a future life. We need not enter into this. It is also supposed that the doctrine runs counter to the idea of man's " responsibility " for his actions. On this point Rosanoff says : " Responsibility, in the sense of liability to profitless retribution for wrong-doing, does not exist, scientifically, in any case. On the other hand, everybody is responsible in the sense of being liable to forfeit his liberty, property, or the results of his labour, when necessary for the protection of the rights of others or for the restoration of damage caused by him ".[1] The doctrine is also supposed to be degrading to man's conception of his mind. It certainly is, in a sense, humbling to that conception. But, to those who grasp it fully, the doctrine is, literally, the most inspiring influence which can be conceived. It comes to explain life anew, and to sweeten the prospect of death. No words are adequate to express the freedom and the happiness of the mind which it produces.

To sum the whole matter up, Freud regards the whole of our psychic life as consisting of a series of wishes or (perhaps better) impulses. These aim at the fulfilment of two principles. The " pleasure principle " manifests itself as the basic principle of the individual in his primitive stage. It " represents the primary, original form of mental activity. . . . Its main object is a demand for the gratification of various desires of a distinctly lowly order. . . It is thus exquisitely egocentric, selfish, personal, anti-social ".[2] It is easy to see how much

[1] " Manual of Psychiatry."
[2] Ernest Jones, " Papers on Psycho-analysis ".

## 78 THE PSYCHOLOGY OF THE CRIMINAL

this pleasure principle weighs with many of our delinquents. The other, the " reality principle ", has for its object the adaptation of the individual to the reality of the world outside. These two principles are in constant conflict. The pleasure principle is constantly (from the earliest stages of extra-uterine life) being modified by the reality principle, and its desires are being hampered and thwarted by the same influence. Hence arise all the various states of conflict and repression, which play so large a part in our psychic life. It is not the author's task to pursue this most fascinating and enormous subject any further. We now turn to the nature of psycho-analysis.

Psycho-analysis is a science. The discovery and the elaboration of this method have been made in a scientific manner. It consists in the investigation of the contents and the mode of working of the unconscious mind, and of the relations of the unconscious with the conscious mind. For, as we have seen, the two are very closely connected. We have already said that perhaps the very last thing which a man desires to understand is himself. This reluctance must be overcome in the interests both of the individual and the race. Schopenhauer has said : " The truth has not been found, not because it was unsought, but because the intention was always to find out again some preconceived opinion, or not to wound some favourite idea." All these preconceived opinions and favourite ideas must be laid aside at the start. Our old explanations have proved quite inadequate. We are starting on the exploration of a new country, and the old maps are not only useless, they are misleading. By psycho-analysis we are able to discover the ultimate origins of much of our conscious mental life. This is the value of psycho-analysis as regards diagnosis. And even if it went no further than this, psycho-analysis would greatly assist us in Court work. For a comprehension of the true roots of human conduct is far more than

# THE OFFENDER'S UNCONSCIOUS MIND 79

we have hitherto possessed. In fact, from a scientific point of view, diagnosis is the important thing, and must be regarded quite apart from its practical applications. But we hope to do far more than this. We aspire to make the future better. We are trying to find a path through a most complicated tangle of undergrowth, to harmonize the elements of mental life, and to restore, if possible, to healthy mental activity those who have been unable to adapt themselves to the requirements of life. We strive " to hold up the weak, to heal the sick, to bind up the broken, and to bring again the out-cast ". This is the great task of psycho-analysis as regards treatment. In many cases the force exerted by civilization on the development of the individual appears to have been too great, and to have been exerted too rapidly. Many of the ills which result from this are amenable to the help of psycho-analysis. We now proceed to describe shortly the technique of this method.

The unconscious mind can be explored in more than one way. Various methods have been adopted.

1. *Hypnotism.* Under certain circumstances the consciousness of an hypnotized subject may be almost entirely obliterated, while his memory for forgotten incidents may be greatly increased. So, on the face of things, it would seem that hypnosis would be the ideal method of psycho-analysis. Freud and most other psycho-analysts have, however, discarded this method. There are obvious objections to the use of hypnosis in Court work. The author has no personal experience of the practice of hypnosis, and he would be most unwilling to use it. We may here mention that treatment by means of *hypnotic suggestion*, though it may be very useful in its own line, has nothing whatever to do with psycho-analysis. Nothing has to be more carefully avoided in psycho-analysis than any trace of suggestion by the psycho-analyst. This point cannot be too clearly understood.

# 80 THE PSYCHOLOGY OF THE CRIMINAL

(2) *Word Association*. The subject sits at ease, and the examiner is seated, preferably behind him. Having obtained the subject's confidence, and induced him to describe as fully as possible the cause of his coming under the examiner's hands, he is directed to allow his mind to wander freely. The idea of the process in question is then explained to him. It consists in the reading by the examiner of a series of words, to each of which the subject is directed to reply by the first *word* which occurs to him. The examiner notes the response (technically known as the " reaction "), and also notes whether the time taken to produce the response is unduly prolonged. The use of a stop-watch has been advised, but the author counts this unnecessary. In practice it will be found quite easy to note prolonged reaction times without the aid of the watch, and the less both examiner and subject are distracted by apparatus the better. The list of words is of some importance. There are several standard lists. That of Kent and Rosanoff is convenient, for the responses from 1,000 " normal " subjects have been recorded and classified.[1] The words should be of an ordinary character and quite short, and should consist mostly of nouns and adjectives. All ambiguity of meaning must be avoided in framing the list. The author included the word " sweet " in his list. This, on one occasion, produced what appeared to be the curious reaction " furniture ". But the matter was explained when it was found that the subject had mistaken the stimulus word for " suite ". It is well to go over the list at more than one sitting. When the test is completed the results should be scrutinized with meticulous care, and note is taken of :—

(*a*) Peculiar reactions.

[1] The list, with tables of reactions, will be found in Rosanoff's " Manual of Psychiatry ". The original monograph appeared in the " American Journal of Insanity ", 1910.

## THE OFFENDER'S UNCONSCIOUS MIND 81

(b) Reactions in which there is prolongation of the reaction time.

(c) Reactions which take the form of repetition of the stimulus word.

(d) Reactions which take the form, not of one word, but of sentences or explanations.

(e) Disturbances of the reactions which follow after some particular stimulus word.

(f) Any physical signs of perturbation of mind accompanying a reaction.

(g) Any different responses to stimulus words, if the list is repeated on more than one occasion.

(Before regarding any reaction as peculiar, be quite certain that the subject has correctly heard and understood the stimulus word.)

The noteworthy reactions are then taken one by one, and the subject is desired to analyse them, and to endeavour to remember how the response came into his mind. He must be urged to suspend all criticism, to allow his mind to wander freely among the associations which present themselves, and not to reject any association because it seems to him to be trivial, ridiculous, or irrelevant. In practice it will be found that these apparently meaningless associations are by far the most important.

The method is of great use. But it is not always the simple thing to apply which some may think. Some subjects seem unable to grasp the idea of what they are wanted to do, and some are probably prevented by the censorship from grasping it. It is, in such a case, quite useless to attempt to force the method. It has been suggested that certain words should be included in the list, such as appear likely to touch the subject's buried complexes. The author strongly deprecates this. If we start by forming our own ideas as to what the subject's repressed complexes are, we are quite certain to be led astray.

## 82 THE PSYCHOLOGY OF THE CRIMINAL

The method is, perhaps, more an introduction to psycho-analysis than psycho-analysis itself. But even taken by itself it has great value. And it may serve to clear up difficulties which might otherwise have prevented any understanding of a case. To take an example, the author had a young girl sent to him who had attempted suicide. She appeared quite unable, and probably was really unable, to give any explanation of her act. She stoutly denied any kind of trouble, and persisted in saying that she had no cause for her attempt. The method of word association produced very marked prolongation of reaction time, and very peculiar reactions to the stimulus words " father ", " wish ", " walk ", " duty ", " obey ", and " man ". Further analysis produced recognition of the fact that she had been anxious to " walk out " with a certain young man, but that her father had forbidden her to do so. As a result, there had been a mental conflict between her desire to go out with the young man and her feeling that it was her duty to obey her father. Not only was this information useful as explaining the attempt at suicide, but the girl's whole life was cleared up. Further investigation of the lover's character induced the father to withdraw his veto, with the happiest results. To take another case, a young married man committed an act of grossly indecent exposure. Investigation by this method showed that he desired to have a child, whereas his wife, from prudential reasons, declined to take the necessary steps. He was anxious not to urge his wife unduly. Hence arose an obvious mental conflict. The repressed desire in this case expressed itself in an offence of a sexual form. But the mode of expression in such a case may not always be of a sexual form. Such an instance of conflict is only one of many. The author is constantly meeting with them. Other instances of a like nature will be mentioned later.

# THE OFFENDER'S UNCONSCIOUS MIND 83

The method of word association has been combined with the taking of simultaneous galvanic records from the subject. The results are full of promise. They have been described in papers by Peterson and Jung,[1] and by Prideaux.[2] The author has no personal knowledge of this modification of the word association method, which is one which can only be carried out in a properly fitted laboratory. Perhaps, also, it is not well to introduce elaborate apparatus in our particular work.

3. *Free Association.* The subject is placed comfortably as before. After preliminary attention has been paid to his own account of his case, he is directed to allow his mind to wander freely, and to suspend all his critical faculties. He is then encouraged to relate every memory or thought which comes to him in connexion with any of his symptoms, disturbed word associations, or dreams (see later). He may say, and probably will say, that his thoughts or memories are trivial, frivolous, or irrelevant. Or there may be signs that the thoughts or memories are painful, and that he is keeping them back for this reason. But he must be urged to reveal them all. For these thoughts and memories are just the ones which are being kept back by the censorship, and so are those which refer to repressed complexes. This procedure will probably be the method of most practical value from our present point of view. Certainly the author has found it to be so in his own experience. The main drawback to this, as to all other forms of psycho-analysis, is the very large amount of time which has, as a rule, to be spent on any given case. Still a start can always be made. After some practice, it is generally soon obvious if a repressed complex is at the root of the trouble, and also whether the subject is really anxious to be free from the influence thereof. This latter point is of the utmost importance. The practical outcome of these findings

[1] " Brain " 1907.    [2] ibid. 1920.

## 84 THE PSYCHOLOGY OF THE CRIMINAL

will be discussed later. Another point may be mentioned here. It is not always the case that any particular psycho-analyst, however skilled and experienced he may be, will be successful with any one particular subject. Some cases appear to be unanalysible by a particular analyst. And in these cases it is clearly waste of time for him to go on.

There are certain cases in which a short analysis is enough to clear up the trouble. One such instance may be recorded. A woman of about sixty years of age got into trouble for an apparently senseless act of damage. An analysis, continued on four successive days, explained the cause of the act. There had been a most distressing sexual experience more than forty years previously. The memory of this had been repressed, and this was the cause of the whole trouble. When the patient realized this, her whole attitude to life was changed. And the matter having been explained to the Court, so far as could be done without divulging the facts which had been discovered, the case was dismissed. Since then, the author's information is that the woman has got on perfectly well. This leads directly to the discussion of another problem. It is obvious that, if psycho-analysis is to be used in Court work, the questions of the confidential relations between the medical examiner and the patient must be considered. Granting that a repressed experience has been found, it is clear that in many cases it cannot be mentioned in Court, or even embodied in a written report. What is the medical examiner to do ? " The truth and nothing but the truth ", must be given in evidence. But it is obvious that it may be very undesirable to tell " the whole truth." And unless the position is made clear to the patient at the outset, it will be useless to attempt any form of psycho-analysis. It seems to the author that the solution is as follows : The Court must know, and must be prepared to place the fullest confidence in,

## THE OFFENDER'S UNCONSCIOUS MIND 85

the examiner who is employed by it. It must be ready to accept his statement that he has discovered a repressed complex which he honestly believes to be the cause of the delinquency, or that he is of opinion that further analysis would be of advantage in throwing more light upon the case, or of benefiting the patient by freeing him from the impulse to commit similar offences. It will then be for the Court to decide what line of action it is to take. (In our final chapter we shall consider the circumstances under which such further analysis could be carried on.) The author's experience in Birmingham indicates that Courts, when they know and trust their examiner, are quite ready to take the view which is put forward here. In the interviews with a patient, or with his relatives, or with his legal adviser, it may be well (while laying stress upon the complete inviolability as to facts discovered during the examination) to discuss what he or they may think it desirable that the Court should know.

4. *The Interpretation of Dreams.* Freud calls this method " the royal road to the unconscious ". And for a full account of his theory the reader is referred to his original work.[1] But the subject is of such intense interest and importance that some account of it must be given here. The study and the interpretation of dreams has, of course, been practised for ages past. But it was left for Freud to place the matter on a scientific basis. He has shown that every dream is the fulfilment of conscious or unconscious wishes, and that what may appear to be exceptions to this general rule are not so in reality. He shows that the dream makes use of incidents of our waking experience for this purpose. The dream elements are more or less distorted. And the degree of this distortion varies as the wish of which the dream is the imaginary fulfilment is more or less acceptable to the waking conscious.

[1] " The Interpretation of Dreams ", translated by A. A. Brill.

## 86 THE PSYCHOLOGY OF THE CRIMINAL

(This is the reason why the dreams of children are so much less distorted than are those of adults.) If a wish is unacceptable to consciousness it is repressed into the unconscious. And so, in order to pass the censorship, which exists during sleep, although doubtless it is somewhat relaxed then, the imaginary fulfilment has to be disguised. Sexual wishes, under the conditions of modern civilization, are the most repressed of all. And so sexual wishes form the basis of most, perhaps of all, dreams.

In every dream there is what is known as a " manifest " and a " latent " content. The former consists of the dream incidents as we might relate them, and as in fact some of us do relate them, to a friend next morning. The latent content is the deeper, hidden meaning, which we are only able to discover by means of the association of the various dream items. This latent content always proves to be the fulfilment of a wish. By dreaming we gratify unconscious desires which would, if gratified in any other way, produce mental disturbance. Should the latent content of a dream become ineffectively disguised, the result is that we awake. So the disguise of the wish is designed to protect sleep. The object of our dreams is " to keep the gates of sleep," as Swinburne has poetically put it. The dream protects sleep by stilling the activity of unconscious mental processes which would otherwise act as disturbing agents.

There are certain aspects of dream distortion to which technical names have been given :

(a) *Displacement.* One idea is substituted for another. And what appear to be quite trivial items in the dream are usually the most important.

(b) *Condensation.* Dream elements may contain a number of unconscious thoughts which have become, in a way, fused together.

(c) *Symbolization.* This occurs far more often in dreams than in waking life, although it is made use of

# THE OFFENDER'S UNCONSCIOUS MIND 87

even in waking consciousness. Symbols are the disguises under which the unconscious presents to consciousness those experiences which are denied admission to consciousness, in their proper forms, on account of their painful character. This theory of symbolization has been worked out in great detail. But it is not necessary, perhaps not desirable, to enter into the interpretation of symbolism here. The idea of this chapter is merely to explain the theory upon which psychoanalysis rests, in order to make its possible application to Court work intelligible. The author has no intention of writing a treatise on psycho-analysis. Those who desire further information are referred to the ample and constantly growing literature on the subject.

(d) *Dramatization*. The situations, characters, and incidents in the dream are arranged and combined into a connected whole. Time is, in a sense, obliterated. Many readers will be able to recall the way in which long periods of time seem to be covered in their dreams. The author remembers one occasion when, on waking one morning, he looked at his watch, and found the time to be exactly 7.30. Not being desirous of arising, just then, he " turned over " and went to sleep again. He had a most elaborate dream, in which the events of two entire days passed before his mind with most dramatic detail. He awoke again with the feeling that he had grossly overslept himself, but on consulting his watch found the time to be not quite 7.32. A very similar instance is recorded of the late Dean Stanley. Truly, in the unconscious there is no past (and no forgetting), all is present. " One day is as a thousand years, and a thousand years as one day."

The first step in the interpretation of a dream is to find out what the different items represent. The method adopted for this somewhat resembles the word-association method. Each item of the dream-picture stands in the place of the stimulus word. When the symbolic

## 88 THE PSYCHOLOGY OF THE CRIMINAL

meaning of the various items has been discovered, we then have to try and fit the pieces into a connected whole. No one will feel doubt of the enormous sphere of usefulness which we possess in this method if he will make a trial. Let the most sceptical have some of his dreams analysed by one who is capable of performing the task, and he will be convinced.

When the dream has been partly analysed the inner meaning may have become clear to the analyst. And he then has the temptation to force his own construction on the patient. This must, at all cost, be resisted. It is absolutely necessary that the patient should realize the meaning for himself. The efforts of the analyst must be confined to assisting the patient to achieve this end. " The work of the psycho-analyst is to note and follow up all the spontaneous manifestations and re-actions of the patient, physical and mental. So the patient himself, under the guidance of the psycho-analyst, makes a map of his own psyche. Selection and criticism of the conscious ' intellectual ' mind must be laid aside. The investigation must be quite compre-hensive. The psycho-analyst must not impose his own intellectual and moral judgments on the patient. His part is to guide, to illuminate, to compare, and to break up complexities."[1]

It cannot be too often emphasized that the emotional part of psycho-analysis is the important part. It is far more important than is the intellectual factor. The patient has to re-experience his repressed emotions. Autognosis, knowledge of self, is the object aimed at in the process. The intention is that the patient should understand himself, and should make his own readjustments.

The essential point in psycho-analysis is the discovery and the breaking down of the resistances which have been keeping the repressed complexes in the uncon-

[1] Barbara Low, " Psycho-analysis ".

## THE OFFENDER'S UNCONSCIOUS MIND 89

scious. The psycho-analyst's duty is to do this, or rather, to assist the patient to do it. So it is more important for the psycho-analyst to attend to these resistances than to the particular morbid symptoms of the patient. When the resistances have been broken down, then the complexes will reveal their contents. All this bears out what we have said as to the mistake of paying undue attention to the particular act with which an offender may happen to be charged at any particular time. When a " cure " is effected by means of psycho-analysis it is effected by bringing into consciousness complexes which were the basis of the symptoms. This process is known as " psychical catharsis " (purging). When the patient realizes what the basis of his symptoms is, he will be assisted in making more normal adjustments to reality. His symptoms were a pathological adjustment. And so in any " cure " by psycho-analysis there are three steps. (1) We have to discover the repressed complex, and to bring it into consciousness. (A complex may be regarded as a set of emotions grouped around a nucleus [a person, an event, a memory, etc.]). (2) We have to detach the nucleus from its surrounding emotions. (3) We cannot get rid of the nucleus, so we have to surround it with a fresh set of emotions, and to divert the original emotions into fresh channels, " sublimate " them, as it is termed.

It is speciously urged by some that the psycho-analyst must guide the patient's sublimation, that the analysis must have a constructive side. Tempting as this is (for the desire to direct other people is present in all of us) it must, in the author's opinion, be sternly resisted. It can only end in the psycho-analyst enforcing his own views, as to conduct, on the patient.

We have to mention a subject of importance known as " transference ". By this term is meant the displacement, which occurs during the process of psycho-analysis, of various feelings, appertaining to some other

## 90 THE PSYCHOLOGY OF THE CRIMINAL

person, on to the psycho-analyst. Characteristics of speech, manner, etc. in the analyst tend unconsciously to remind the patient of some other person or persons. As a result, the patient identifies the analyst with these other persons. And the feelings of the patient with regard to these persons (and the feelings may be friendly or hostile) are said to be transferred to the analyst. We have pointed out that the essential feature of a cure by psycho-analysis is that the patient must re-experience his repressed emotions. He must, therefore, connect them with some person, and that person is the analyst. So the patient will contend that his re-experienced feelings are reactions to the analyst's conduct towards him (the patient). The task of the analyst, and it may be the most difficult part of his work, is to make the patient realize how these feelings have been produced.

It will be seen that psycho-analysis is a method of great difficulty, requiring knowledge of a special technique, much experience, and perhaps certain gifts which are not possessed by all. It is a trying process for the patient. It involves renunciation, and this is never easy. It is still more trying for the psycho-analyst. Until an attempt has been made, no one can conceive what a severe strain this method is. It is additionally hard because the analyst may not feel in the mood for undertaking it. And yet circumstances may render its undertaking necessary.

It may be mentioned here that other theories of the operation of the unconscious mind have been elaborated by certain of Freud's followers, who, after going some way with the great pioneer, have branched off in other directions. No analysis of their views can be attempted here. But we may mention the theories of Adler and of Jung. Adler's theory seems to represent the mind as the seat of conflict between " masculine " and " feminine " tendencies ; in other words, between the self-assertive and the submissive tendencies. On this view, there

# THE OFFENDER'S UNCONSCIOUS MIND 91

is a constant attempt to rectify some part of his character in which the subject feels himself to be deficient. Phantasy often takes the form of a compensatory effort at self-assertion.

Jung's theory considers the unconscious as consisting of two parts. There is a " collective " unconscious, which is the experience of the race, and which is specially liable to express itself in symbolic modes of thought ; and there is also a " personal " unconscious, derived from the subject's individual experiences. If we adopted this theory, it might be tempting to consider the criminal as one in whom the racial unconscious is unduly prominent ; and this was, in effect, what Lombroso held. Jung agrees with Freud in retaining the ideas of conflict resulting in repression, or in mental trauma. According to Jung, dreaming is the activity of the deeper, the older parts of the mind, the upper parts of the mind being asleep. So that we think in dreams as our remote ancestors thought (of course, elements from our own recent experiences come in as well). According to Jung, a dream has not only a past, but also a future significance. (Even on Freud's theory a dream may be prospective. For if a large part of our mind is expressing itself in dreams, it must mean that this part is likely to assume a dominant position.) Jung drops the idea of the censorship. And the essential part of his theory is that the psychic energy (" libido ") is purposive, teleological. This is where he differs from Freud, whose theory is deterministic. And this difference is quite fundamental. Jung recognizes this, and he calls his method " analytical psychology ", to mark its distinction from the method of Freud. Jung's theory appears to be gaining popularity in this country. The author feels that this is largely due to an unconscious objection to the acceptance of Freud's theory of psychical determinism. There appears to be no way of reconciling the two views. Either a man

## 92 THE PSYCHOLOGY OF THE CRIMINAL

accepts the doctrine of psychical determinism or he does not. Argument on the subject is probably quite useless. But the author cannot refrain from again expressing his own, personal adherence to the Freudian theory. And this book is written throughout on a deterministic basis.

Certain difficulties may arise in psycho-analysis on account of the attitude of the patient. It has already been explained that, in a sense, the patient treats himself; that the physician acts as a guide in assisting the patient to obtain a comprehension of his own (the patient's) mind. So the difficulties of which we are now speaking are obstacles which the patient raises unconsciously; and not deliberate, conscious resistances. If the latter form of resistance is met with, then it is obviously useless to proceed further with the psycho-analysis. This last point must be kept in mind in relation to Court work. For it happens that a patient sometimes does not desire to be free from the influence of his mental conflict. The desire to be free from the conflict is quite different from the desire to escape from the legal consequences of a particular delinquent action. Just so, we get the case of a pensioner who does not wish to be free from a neurosis, because that freedom would imply the removal of his pension.

We may have the patient who is over anxious to help, who is always saying, " What am I to do ? ". He has to be told that he is not wanted to " do " anything, that his task is just to let his thoughts run freely and without control. Or we may have the patient who produces a mighty flood of associations, which are really, though unconsciously, intended to cover up some complex which his unconscious mind desires to conceal. This type of patient the author has found to be very common among those who are accused of a sexual form of delinquency. Then we have the patient who, having given a number of associations, comes to a stop and says he cannot

# THE OFFENDER'S UNCONSCIOUS MIND 93

remember anything more. A block of this kind is of much importance, for it indicates that we have arrived at the outworks of the citadel, and that the censorship has become active. Or again, the patient may hesitate and show that he is obviously keeping back associations. He may say, when questioned, that the concealed associations are too trivial, ridiculous, or irrelevant to mention. We may then be quite certain that these particular associations are actually of the greatest importance, and we must urge the patient to reveal everything, without exception. In fact, a patient's failures to react are quite as important as his reactions, and sometimes are more important. Quite apart from psycho-analysis, may not this rule apply to the whole subject of a man's conduct? Not only must we consider how he has reacted to the stimuli of society, but also how he has failed to react. The important matter consists of what a man *is*, and this is shown by what he has left undone, as well as by what he has done.

So long as associations are allowed to form *freely*, a repressed complex appears to possess a kind of magnetic attraction.

A patient may assume an attitude of impersonal, scientific interest in the proceedings. This is a form of unconscious resistance, and is more common among intelligent patients. This brings us to the question whether intelligent patients are the most suitable for our purpose of psycho-analysis. The view of some psycho-analysts of much experience is that intelligent subjects are the best to deal with, and that lack of intelligence is a great handicap to the method. If this opinion be correct, it will limit the application of psycho-analysis in Court work. The author, however, has had some success in dealing with subjects who were far from being highly intelligent. He has found, for instance, that it may be helpful to attempt the interpretation of dreams in such subjects. This is especially the case

## 94 THE PSYCHOLOGY OF THE CRIMINAL

when we get such patients young. The author has often had to forgo psycho-analysis in some particular patient, from lack of time, due to a short sentence. And there is a vast scope for work on these lines in institutions where suitable young patients are detained for sufficiently long periods.

The author has attempted to give a short account of the theory and the methods of psycho-analysis. He knows that his exposition has been meagre and superficial. But he trusts that he has made it intelligible. We can now pass on to a fuller consideration of the application of psycho-analysis to the elucidation of the problems with which Courts are faced in their daily work.

CHAPTER IV

# THE OFFENDER'S UNCONSCIOUS MIND
### (*Continued*)

THE theory of the unconscious mind introduces us to a new realm of thought as regards man's conduct, and so it profoundly modifies our conceptions of delinquency.

We have seen that psycho-analysis is the scientific study of human motives. Conduct is the direct result of mental life. Every action which a man performs, every word which he speaks (for words are but spoken conduct, the distinction between " words " and " deeds " is only superficial) is the result of some psychical process. We can have no knowledge of human conduct, in the sense of understanding it, until we learn about the mental processes which underlie it. Psycho-analysis is the scientific study of motives. The whole method rests upon the fact that to understand human motives we must investigate the mental experiences of early life, whatever may have been the source of these experiences. The importance of this was, of course, recognized long before Freud's day. It is very interesting to read in Oliver Wendell Holmes's " Autocrat " written in 1850, the following words : " The first instinctive movement of children is to make a *cache*, and bury in it beliefs, doubts, dreams, hopes, and terrors." He could hardly have written more accurately from the psycho-analytic point of view. Freud has but shown that we must trace the patient's mental processes further back than was formerly considered either necessary or

## 96 THE PSYCHOLOGY OF THE CRIMINAL

possible. If we trace back the mental causes of conduct in any individual, we find their origins so far away, that the links in the chain of causation are not easily discovered.

In considering conduct we see many instances of the operation of our primitive tendencies. We have the varieties of the "collecting instinct". And this instinct, combined with the well-known attraction of bright objects for primitive man, goes far to explain many cases of "hotel thefts". Again, the instinct of "trusting to chance" is common among savages: hence we have stock exchange transactions and other forms of gambling. There is contained in the unconscious of all of us many tendencies which are the remains of primitive and uncivilized life. No doubt this is the reason why remedial measures fail in so many cases. Society has developed by very slow degrees. Many of our most elementary instincts have had to be repressed in order to fit us for life in society. With many of us, perhaps with most of us, these instincts have been sufficiently repressed. But we have but to consider what has recently happened in Russia to see how strong these instincts are, and how close they lie to the surface. And many of the happenings in all countries during the war point in the same direction. With some persons these instincts have never been really repressed. Lombroso was not far wrong when he regarded the "criminal" as an atavistic survival. Primitive man would have been quite unfitted for life in society as we know that organization. And the survival of the primitive type, with quite unrepressed instincts, is the explanation of some of our "habitual criminals". The bearing of this position, so far as concerns the treatment of offenders, is obvious. And in the concluding chapter of this book we shall point out the necessity of permanent detention for some of these cases. Regular and steady work, and co-opera-

## THE OFFENDER'S UNCONSCIOUS MIND 97

tion with his fellows, would have been quite an impossible task for primitive man, and it is so for some of our offenders to-day. Psycho-analysis teaches us how fine is the line between what we regard as " normal " and as " abnormal ". We must not think of the sexual or other form of offender as of one who has evolved something new and strange, but as of one who is actuated by the same motives as ourselves, although the resultant of these motives and the manner of their expression may be different.

The mind has evolved by steps which have been forgotten, and along roads which are now lost in the unconscious. Psycho-analysis essentially means retracing the steps which have resulted in the formation of character. We need say no more than this to indicate its immense value for those who study delinquency. Until quite recently, human conduct was very imperfectly understood. And people were obliged to " explain " it, in the absence of any comprehension of its true causes, by making " rationalizations ". And our method of dealing with offenders is still very largely the result of these rationalizations. As a result of our increased knowledge of the causes of delinquency it may be expected that our estimation of offenders, and our reaction towards them, will be radically altered. To say this is not to blame our predecessors. Their reaction towards offenders was the only possible one in the light of their imperfect knowledge.

Mental conflicts and the resulting repressions are among the main causative factors which produce delinquent conduct. The complexity and the subtlety of mental processes is exceedingly deep. This depth has not yet been fully measured, perhaps, never can be so measured. We are but beginning to use the sounding line, and we are just commencing to realize what the depth really is. Psycho-analysis is teaching us how deepseated, how distant, and how apparently unconnected

## 98 THE PSYCHOLOGY OF THE CRIMINAL

with the action, the real cause thereof may be. R. C. Lehmann, in his amusing papers, " The Adventures of Picklock Holes," makes his hero trace the connecting links between the two ideas, " hat-band " and " archbishop ". But this train of thought, which was intended when penned, thirty years ago, to be farcical, would be quite common-place to-day, as anyone who has made a trial of psycho-analysis will know. No one who desires to make a study of any individual offender can afford to neglect the attempt to track down the delinquent action to its original source. He will find himself repaid a thousandfold for the expenditure of time and trouble which is entailed. And he will, at first, be surprised at the frequency with which he will find some mental conflict to be at the base of the whole trouble.

The existence of a mental conflict naturally involves great emotional disturbance. Now men and women, like other animals, are so constituted that nothing arouses such profound emotions as sex matters, taking the term " sex " in the wide sense in which it is used by Freud, who includes, under this heading, authority, attraction, friendliness, modesty, shame, and disgust. So it would appear likely that we should discover some sex element at the basis of many emotional disturbances, and such, in fact, we find is the case. We need not enter into the discussion as to whether there is a sex element at the basis of *all* emotional disturbances. We may content ourselves with the assumption, which will probably be generally accepted, that there often is this basis. When we reflect how deep-seated and how important is the sex instinct, and how much this instinct is repressed, confined, and thwarted, by the forces of modern civilization, we can easily see why it gives rise to so much of mental conflict. We constantly find the causes of such a conflict to gather around early sex experiences, or around repressed sexual thoughts and images. In thus speaking of such sex experiences, we

## THE OFFENDER'S UNCONSCIOUS MIND 99

must not suppose them to have been always physical and personal. There have often been experiences in the environment. Sometimes, of course, the connexion between the sex experiences and the particular form of delinquency which results therefrom is easily discovered and apparent. No surprise will be felt at the position that there is often a sex basis for the adoption of a life of prostitution by a girl, or for acts of indecent assault, or exposure on the part of a man. And the author need not labour this point further. But many other and widely different forms of delinquency may result from such a sex complex. We may use Healy's term, and say that there are such things as "substitution delinquencies". It would seem as if the repressed emotion expresses itself in action in diverse ways. Unable to escape by one door, it gets out by another. The emotion gives rise to a sense of tension, and this tension finds relief when the emotion discovers some way of expressing itself in action. Nor need we wonder. It is well known to neurologists that a repressed complex may result in what is known as an " anxiety neurosis ", or in what is called an hysterical symptom (e.g. some form of paralysis). And we shall have some remarks to make on these points later. So it would seem, on the face of things, quite likely that such a repressed complex should issue into consciousness in the form of a desire to commit some particular act. It is on a footing with the well-known instances in which a repressed desire to scream from the effects of physical pain finds issue in muscular action (clenching the fists, or fiercely biting on something), or where the impulse of rage, baulked of its natural outlet, finds issue in the act of smashing furniture ; or of deliberate unkindness to some person who is quite unconnected with the real occasion of the rage.

The mental conflicts which may be discovered, and the delinquencies which may result therefrom, are of

# 100 THE PSYCHOLOGY OF THE CRIMINAL

almost infinite variety. This alone is enough to remove the charge of monotony which is often brought against work with offenders. No doubt the work would be monotonous if we merely looked at the offences which our patients are alleged to have committed. But the charge of sameness is put aside if we attempt to investigate further into the cause of the offences. Of the many instances which have come under his notice the author selects a few examples :—

1. A patient had been separated from his wife for many years, but had remained continent. Repression of sexual desire resulted in a complex which issued in the form of indecent assaults upon small girls, although he was fond of, and generally kind to, children.

2. Normal sexual desires may be baulked of their outlet through ignorance or nervousness. In one instance of this kind the resulting repressed complex issued in the form of indecent assault, in another similar case it issued in the form of larceny.

3. A repressed complex in a man originated from his family looking down upon his wife on account of her having been immoral before marriage. The resulting delinquency took the form of larceny, the unconscious desire being to put himself on a level with his wife in the eyes of his family by the commission of an offence.

4. A complex may be caused by depression over a trifling and sometimes imaginary physical defect. And this has resulted in one case in an attempt at suicide, and in another in the form of larceny.

5. In a girl, a complex originated in the discovery of the fact that her mother was living in adultery. The result was an attempt at suicide.

6. A man hears casually, that his father had committed suicide when he (the patient) was a child. The mother had previously told him another story about the father's death. The result was an offence of indecent assault.

# THE OFFENDER'S UNCONSCIOUS MIND 101

7. A man is caused what might appear to most people a petty annoyance by another man. The result was larceny from a quite unconnected person.

There is little doubt in the author's mind that in the majority of cases a repressed complex will be found to have a sex basis. And the resulting conflict may give rise to all kinds of offences. We may have stealing of every variety, violent assault, arson. And one striking point must be mentioned. The trouble which such conduct will give the offender may be, and often is, foreseen. This trouble may be very great, and yet the offence may be repeated again and again. Whenever a case is one in which the repetition of suffering should be readily anticipated, it should be marked down as deserving of the most patient and minute investigation.

It is necessary for us to consider certain objections which have been taken to the practice of psycho-analysis.

1. It is said that the psycho-analytic theory lays undue stress upon the sex element in mental life. The term " sexual " is used by Freud in a very extended sense, and we have just mentioned what he includes under this heading. But he so includes these emotions because he realizes that they are, essentially, sexual in origin. When he speaks of " sexual " actions in a child, or of infantile " sexual " desires, he does not suggest that these are, in the child, consciously sexual. He means that we should certainly regard them as sexual if they occurred in an adult. When we consider the enormous part which the sex instinct plays ; when we remember the importance of this instinct in the art, literature, and drama of all ages ; when we consider the influence which this instinct has upon those around us in our daily life, we shall hardly be disposed to underrate it. The part which this instinct plays in the production of the neuroses has been demonstrated beyond all cavil. And it is clear that it is of vast importance in the abnormal mind. This is the type

## 102 THE PSYCHOLOGY OF THE CRIMINAL

of mind with which we are chiefly called upon to deal in Court work. It is not necessary, for our present purpose, to discuss whether the sex instinct is of similar importance in the " normal " mind.

2. Psycho-analysis is not a branch of practice which all are qualified to take up. This is undoubtedly true. The study appeals in the first instance to a special type of mind. The psycho-analyst must possess an adequate knowledge of general medicine. Then he must have acquired a knowledge of his own speciality. He needs to know much of the human heart and of its " dark " places. He requires ample sympathy and unwearied patience. He must endeavour to free himself from all trammels of prejudice, whether social, " moral ", or religious. This freedom of mind can be attained to a greater degree than some might imagine to be possible. He must dismiss from his mind all desire to judge or to blame. These qualifications are certainly not possessed by all. But other specialities are equally limited. It is not necessary for us to condemn cataract operations because their performance demands a skill and an experience which are not found among general practitioners. The general practitioner knows, or should know, that certain cases of cataract are benefited by operative measures, and he sends such cases to an oculist. So let it be with psycho-analysis. It does not seem necessary that the student of psycho-analysis should adopt any particular view as to the relation between physical and psychical processes, for the theory of psycho-analysis is compatible with several of these theories. But it does seem well that the student should have some knowledge as to what theories have been, and are held as to these relations, and that he should adopt that one which most commends itself to his mind. For an analysis of these theories in a reasonably brief form see McDougall.[1] The author may perhaps be

[1] " Body and Mind."

## THE OFFENDER'S UNCONSCIOUS MIND 103

allowed to say that the particular form of psycho-physical parallelism enunciated by Spinoza is the most attractive to him. We have seen reason to think that the Freudian analyst must be a strict determinist.

3. Not all cases are suitable for psycho-analysis, or are curable by that mode of treatment. But the claim that all cases are so curable has never been made. Later in this book an attempt is made to define what, from our present point of view, the probable limitations of this method are.

4. Psycho-analysis may do harm. It certainly may in unskilled or unscrupulous hands. So may a surgical operation. But this is no valid objection to its use by proper persons.

5. That the last stage of the patient may be worse than the first, that the place of a formerly repressed complex may be taken by another. This generally means that the analysis has not been carried deeply enough. There may be several repressed complexes, super-imposed, so to speak, upon each other. The "upper-most" complex may have dominated the situation, and may have escaped into consciousness in the form of some symptom. Bringing this complex into consciousness may simply have given opportunity for some "under-lying" complex to produce some other symptom. But even if the objection were true it is surely no reason for not attempting the cure of one ill that the patient may, later on, suffer from some other ill. It is hard, however, to see how the performance of a proper psycho-analysis can be productive of anything but good.

6. That bringing to consciousness a complex formerly repressed may result in the patient's acting in accordance with the "dictates" of that complex. This is not confirmed by experience. If the inhibiting forces have been strong enough to prevent a complex from becoming conscious, surely they must be strong enough to control it when it has been brought into consciousness.

## 104 THE PSYCHOLOGY OF THE CRIMINAL

Psycho-analysis liberates the complexes from the unconscious, but not that they may have unrestricted liberty. The complexes are brought into consciousness in order that, being recognized, they may be controlled and that the psychic energy attached to them may be turned to desired and desirable ends. Psycho-analysis aims at inducing a knowledge of self. This knowledge can never place a man at a disadvantage. Better that he should know what his buried complexes are, and not have them breaking out in just the direction in which he happens to be weakest, as is the case when they exist in the unconscious. Obtaining a knowledge of self can never be anything but painful. It is only by sacrifice, however, that we can attain new birth. Only " through great tribulation " can we enter into the Kingdom. It is the truth which alone can make us free. " Thou requirest truth in the inward parts, and thou shalt make me to understand wisdom secretly." The essential thing is that a man should understand himself, not that he should be informed about himself by another.

7. That there are dangers in the practice to the psycho-analyst himself. There may be this drawback, but it exists in other lines of medical work. The remedy is for the analyst to be a person of character and discretion. The fact that the medical profession is under some form of control is a reason for restricting the practice of psycho-analysis to medical practitioners.

8. That it consists of treatment by what is known as suggestion. This objection arises from an entire misconception of the nature of psycho-analysis. Suggestion is never made by the psycho-analyst to the patient. Even the sexual suggestions, when they occur, are always introduced by the patient. Psycho-analysis does not consist in any mere " talking over " of the patient's symptoms, or of any kind of " confession ". It is not so much a question of the patient remembering incidents in his past life, the memory of which has been

## THE OFFENDER'S UNCONSCIOUS MIND 105

repressed ; it is a matter of his re-experiencing the emotions connected with these incidents.

9. That the result may be undue dependence of the patient on the psycho-analyst. This will not occur if the psycho-analysis is properly done.

10. That the process takes a large amount of time. This is certainly true. But it is surely no valid objection to a scientific mode of treatment, except in the eyes of those who always desire " quick returns ". If the results justify the treatment, then all requirements are satisfied. When the benefits of psycho-analysis are fully understood, then the workers will be found. But, as said before, we shall hope for the best results from the younger patients, in whom there is more mental pliancy, and in whom we have not to explore so far. Hence in these cases less time will be wanted.

It is a remarkable thing that most of the objections to psycho-analysis are taken by those who know least about the subject. It is curious that even some very eminent persons have condemned psycho-analysis when they have been, by their own confession, entirely ignorant on the matter. In no branch of science can we allow the estimation of the results obtained to be conducted by those who know nothing of the science or of its methods. Many objections, however, are nothing but pretexts used for the purpose of covering other and deeper objections. Though it may well be that those who bring the objections are unconscious of the real roots of their hostility.

A great difficulty in psycho-analysis is that the analyst has trouble in penetrating into the mind of another because he has not yet passed the barriers which exist between his own consciousness and unconsciousness. It is this which renders it so highly desirable that the analyst should, if possible, undergo a thorough analysis himself. Until the barriers between his own consciousness and unconsciousness have been passed, the would-be

8

## 106 THE PSYCHOLOGY OF THE CRIMINAL

examiner has not the qualifications necessary to see into the unconscious mind of another. He does not wish to see those elements in the other's mind which have been repressed into his own unconscious. This is the reason why some opponents of psycho-analysis say that they have studied the minds of others and have failed to find what the psycho-analysts say they have found. It is probable that these critics know nothing of their own unconscious mind. And so they will fail to find their way into the unconscious mind of another.

The original therapeutic application of psycho-analysis was made in the treatment of the two groups of diseases which are known as the " neuroses ". There is much in these diseases which must be considered in connexion with delinquency. And the causation of these diseases and the application of psycho-analysis to their investigation and treatment has many points in common with the theory suggested as to the cause and treatment of some forms of delinquency. So some words must be said on this head.

1. Neurasthenia. This disease is characterized by abnormal susceptibility to fatigue upon slight exertion. In many cases the disease appears to have an hereditary basis. It was once supposed that the patient's store of nervous energy had been " squandered by his ancestors ". But parents can affect their offspring in other ways than by inheritance. And it is likely that the correct view is that the conduct of the parents towards the child during his early life is responsible for his failure to make proper adjustments to reality. (There is much reason to think that neurasthenia is always due to repressed auto-eroticism, i.e. erotic feelings generated within the subject and directed towards himself.) The patient complains of fatigue on the very least exertion, mental or physical. Even the idea of work may be most repulsive. There is failure of the power of attention, and defect of volition. Psycho-

# THE OFFENDER'S UNCONSCIOUS MIND 107

analysis is the only form of treatment which offers any hope of permanent cure. The marked likeness between the symptoms indicated above, and those presented by many offenders will be obvious. But, quite apart from this, it is clear that persons who suffer from neurasthenia are very likely to fall into delinquency when confronted with the stress of ordinary life. Of course it need hardly be mentioned that a careful physical examination must be made in order to exclude the possibility of some of the symptoms being due to physical disease.

2. The Anxiety Neurosis. This disease is due to sexual excitations which are unable, or which are not permitted, to ensue in either bodily satisfaction or the conscious desire for this satisfaction. The desire is repressed and its place is taken in consciousness by fear, i.e. by the opposite of desire. The fear is not necessarily fear of the particular object which is desired in the unconscious. The main symptom is a general feeling of anxiety. The most ordinary incidents are misinterpreted, and very slight emergencies give rise to alarm, while real danger gives rise to most exaggerated terror. A number of these cases have come under the author's care. Many of them may be cured by psychoanalysis.

3. Hysteria and the Compulsion Neurosis are occasioned not by any presently existing conditions, but by events or phantasies which have occurred in early life. These have been repressed, or an attempt at repression has been made. And they now make their appearance in consciousness in a symbolic form.

In hysteria we have a tendency to dissociation of the personality. Freud's view is that the hysterical symptom represents, symbolically, a compromise between an unconscious wish and its conscious repression. At the outset there is some mental or physical injury

## 108 THE PSYCHOLOGY OF THE CRIMINAL

which excites an abnormal reaction in the patient on account of his early experiences. Soldiers in the firing-line were all exposed to much the same shocks, but only a limited number developed hysterical symptoms. So there must be some other condition acting as well. The circumstances which provoked the hysterical symptoms possess some symbolic value for the patient on account of some former experience which he has repressed, or tried to repress. Hysteria may present either physical symptoms (" conversion hysteria "), such as paralysis, anæsthesia, etc., or mental symptoms (" anxiety hysteria ") where the symptoms are mainly those of anxiety or fear. Or we may have mixed cases. Hysterical subjects are elated or annoyed by trifles. They are egotistic and are always trying to get sympathy from others. And, if they fail to obtain sympathy they will exaggerate their symptoms, or make false statements. The only real cure is psycho-analysis, which uncovers the unconscious conflicts and reveals them to the subject. But the process is as difficult a one as can be imagined.

On the face of things one would expect hysterical subjects to become frequent offenders. But for some reason this is not the case. The author has not seen any large number of hysterical delinquents, and this is the experience of other authorities (e.g. Healy). The general view is that the hysterical subject is incapable of carrying out any act which involves the exercise of much determination. And the author is disposed to agree with this dictum, although there are exceptions to it.

The view is put forward by Rosanoff[1] that hysteria and " malingering " are one and the same condition regarded from two different standpoints, in the one case medical and in the other legal. There is much to be said for this.

[1] op. cit.

## THE OFFENDER'S UNCONSCIOUS MIND 109

The hysteric and the petty criminal are, however, closely allied. In both cases we have the desire to live on others, to draw a pension or dole, and not to be obliged to work. Both classes will steal anything which may be handy, and which can be taken without effort. They will cheat and lie, and are indifferent to the trouble which they cause for others. Certain criminals have, however, the energy to carry out such an offence as a burglary. The hysteric and the petty offender will not do this: it too closely resembles work. Nothing is more common than the remark made by many an offender (referring to his sentence), " This is what I get after fighting for my country." As if fighting for his country gave him the right to live at the expense of his fellow-countrymen for the remainder of his life. But for this attitude the offender is not wholly to blame. The exaggerated and fulsome language used by many, even by those in very high places, during the war has much to answer for in this respect.

There is also what is called the Compulsion Neurosis. Some particular thought or impulse predominates to an almost incontrollable degree. And there are mental conditions in which the subject feels impelled to do certain things " against his will ". Impulses to touch posts in passing, to count the windows in houses, to read notices, etc., are well known. Certain forms of these impulses are of considerable importance in Court work.

1. There is what is popularly known as " kleptomania ". The word is often used very loosely, and as connoting simply excessive stealing. If we are to use the term kleptomania at all it must be carefully defined as meaning the stealing of objects which are apparently of little value to the stealer, and must be distinguished from stealing which is due to what may be termed the " collecting instinct ", and also from the stealing which may occur in some cases of insanity and of mental defect.

# 110 THE PSYCHOLOGY OF THE CRIMINAL

It may, in fact, be termed " pathological stealing ", just as we may speak of " pathological lying" (see Chap. V).

In the author's experience a repressed mental conflict is always to be found in these cases, and this conflict is always of a sex character. These cases are examples of the process in which a repressed sex conflict results in action of an (apparently) non-sexual character. It follows from this that psycho-analysis is the only treatment.

2. In dipsomania again we get periodic outbreaks of excessive drinking, with indifference or aversion to alcohol during the intervals. Here also we have probably always a repressed sex conflict, and psycho-analysis should be tried. Dipsomania must be most carefully distinguished from ordinary chronic alcoholism, with which it is often confused.

3. Homicidal impulses, sometimes directed against a man's or woman's own children, may also occur. In this class of irresistible impulses, the impulse is, at first, resisted, the resistance gives rise to mental pain, the resistance is usually ineffective, the performance of the act is followed by a sense of relief. In all these cases there has been a conflict in early life which has given rise to a repression. This conflict has produced the mental attitude of doubt and uncertainty. Probably the repressed complex is always of a sex character. The emotional energy of the repressed complex has become detached and transferred to something in consciousness. But the obsession to which it is transferred represents a very great distortion of the repressed complex, just as we get distortion in dreams, as described earlier. The treatment is psycho-analysis.

The interest and importance of these conditions to the student of delinquency require no demonstration. Courts are generally somewhat unwilling, and no doubt justly so, to accept a plea of " irresistible impulse " as

## THE OFFENDER'S UNCONSCIOUS MIND 111

an explanation of an offence. But we must recognize that such states do exist. And in certain cases such as kleptomania and repeated arsons, or any other case in which the misconduct is quite out of proportion to any discernible end in view, it would be well to consider whether the explanation of these conditions which has just been given may not be the true one.

Freud's position is that the psychic conflicts which lie at the basis of all neurotic conditions occur in the development of every individual, and this without exception. On the result of these conflicts depends whether any individual will be neurotic or not. It is not that the neurotic individual has been subjected to a conflict from which the healthy individual has been free. The point is, that the two have reacted in different ways to similar conflicts. The process starts in childhood. When an infant arrives in the world, he has none of those social conventions which play so large a part in the life of the adult. The infant is essentially egotistic. He attempts to satisfy his desires whenever and wherever he pleases. He has no sense of the rights of other people, nor does he comprehend the fact that his desires have to be regulated in accordance with those rights. The unconscious has a constant tendency to draw man back to the Nirvana of intrauterine life in which everything was provided for him. This is, of course, why idleness has such an attraction for the majority of people, although this attraction varies in different cases. The connexion of this with delinquency is clear. May this tendency also not account, to some extent, for the great attraction which the idea of the state as a universal provider has for so many of us? The infant's education begins with learning to subdue his personal wishes to the wishes of others, that is to say, he begins to appreciate the reality-principle. Education, in fact, consists of a constant adjustment of conflicts. Impulses have to be given up, and these

## 112 THE PSYCHOLOGY OF THE CRIMINAL

impulses are of far greater importance to the child than is generally recognized. The result of this process is always a compromise. And this compromise may be very imperfect, and may only be attained at the cost of considerable injury to psychical health. In a healthy person this series of conflicts has resulted in the substitution of the original and personal impulses by social ones. The psychic energy of the original impulses furnishes the energy for the later social impulses. So the normal, the healthy process, consists of repression, but of repression accompanied by satisfactory substitution. In the neurotic we have repression also. But in this case the repression is accompanied by unsatisfactory substitution. May we not say that this occurs in the delinquent also ? The satisfactory substitution of the original impulses is known as " sublimation ". The energy which was originally attached to personal desires has been turned into an impersonal direction. In a neurosis the symptoms form a compromise between the unrestrained expression of the original desires and their sublimation. And so, before a cure can be effected, the attachment of the impulses to the symptoms has to be destroyed. A neurosis essentially means that the subject thereof is unconsciously holding on to certain infantile desires. These desires have been repressed. The neurotic symptoms are an expression of the resulting conflict, a means by which the subject obtains an indirect, a symbolical, satisfaction of his infantile desires. So the cure of a neurosis implies a giving up by the subject. He has to divert his interest from the infantile desires, and to devote it to other, to external, objects. And so we have to remember this point. Only one part of the subject's mind, the conscious part, desires a cure. While another part of his mind, the unconscious part, equally strongly desires to remain as before. The subject is in a state of conflict, and from this state his neurosis results, as

## THE OFFENDER'S UNCONSCIOUS MIND 113

said above. Surely all this applies most directly to many cases of delinquency.

Freud himself puts it thus—"It is not the not-knowing in itself that is the pathogenic factor, but the foundation of the not-knowing in internal resistances, which first produced the not-knowing, and still maintains it now. It is in the subduing of these resistances that the therapeutic task lies. . . . If the knowing about his unconscious thoughts were as important for the patient as those inexperienced in psycho-analysis believe, then for a cure it would be enough for the patient to hear lectures or to read books. These measures, however, have as much influence on the nervous sufferings as the distribution of menu cards in a time of famine has upon hunger."[1] And the truth of these remarks has been borne in upon the author in the psychoanalysis which he has attempted with delinquent patients.

In the investigation of any offence, and more especially when that offence has been one of violence, as also in some sexual offences, it will not unfrequently be found that the subject professes complete loss of memory (amnesia) for the events of the offence, and perhaps for the events of the times immediately before and after the offence. He may even fix definite dates and times at which this loss of memory begins and ends. He may say that he remembers doing some definite act, at some named time, that all is a " blank " after that, and that the next thing which he can recall is finding himself at some place at another named time. This is an important feature and must be considered.

In the first place, the loss of memory may be feigned. The subject may have good reason for not desiring to talk about the offence. And this may persist, even when the examiner has taken every precaution in the way of impressing upon the subject that he may talk

[1] " Ueber ' wilde ' Psychoanalyse ".

## 114 THE PSYCHOLOGY OF THE CRIMINAL

with complete freedom, and that facts mentioned by him will be treated in absolute confidence. (In this connexion the author knows that he is dealing with highly controversial matter. Such confidence may be, technically, unknown to the law. But it is absolutely necessary if mental examination is not to be a complete farce. And the author's experience is that this confidence is respected by Courts. He has been told in Court that the medical witness is required to give the opinion which he has formed as to the accused's mental state, that he is not required to reveal any facts as to the offence which the accused may have mentioned to him, indeed he has been specifically warned that he is not to enter into details of conversations which he has held with the accused.)

So the genuineness of the loss of memory is the primary question. No general rules can be laid down as to the decision of this question. Experience comes in to a large extent. The assertion of the same time-limits for the loss of memory at different interviews is an important point.

But having decided that the loss of memory is genuine, under what conditions may it occur ?

1. Epilepsy. Loss of memory for the events of a post epileptic state or of what is called an epileptic " equivalent " is the almost invariable rule. Instances in which there is memory for the events of these states are very exceptional. The question of epilepsy in its general bearing on delinquency will be taken up in the next chapter.

2. Acute Confusional Insanity. This occurs, in predisposed subjects, as a result of intoxication by alcohol and other poisons, during certain acute illnesses of a toxic character, such as influenza or pneumonia, after great exertion or mental anxiety or worry, and sometimes as a result of child-birth. As a rule it will be found that after an attack of this illness there is a

## THE OFFENDER'S UNCONSCIOUS MIND 115

complete blank for the events which have occurred during the illness. In framing such a diagnosis, the other known symptoms of the disease have to be considered. The possibility of a short attack of this form of insanity, lasting a few days, or even a few hours, is sometimes suggested as a defence. Such a suggestion must be received with the greatest caution.

3. In some cases of the Senile Dementia of old age.

4. In certain cases of hysteria.

5. And in some cases, as we have said elsewhere in this book, the desire not to know may produce an actual condition of not knowing. Some experience is so distressing, so out of harmony with the mind as a whole, that the memory of it is repressed into the unconscious, and is maintained there by an active process, quite distinct from what may be termed " passive forgetting ".

Repressed experiences may recover their place in consciousness in the form of some physical symptom. And they may also get back to consciousness in the form of a mental symptom. So it need cause no surprise that they sometimes issue in the shape of a tendency to delinquency. And if we regard the unity of all mental life, and this is perhaps Freud's greatest contribution to knowledge, we shall not be surprised at this smilarity in the causation of the neuroses and of delinquency. Physical and psychical are one, two aspects of the same thing (two sides of the shield), two modes of expression of the same essential reality.

It is no easy task, at the present time, to convince a Court of the reality of these mental conflicts, and of their importance in the causation of offences. We need not wonder at this. Knowledge on this subject is, as yet, very limited, even among medical practitioners. And it will take time before the conservative legal mind is ready to grasp all that the science of psycho-analysis implies. Perhaps it is as well that we should go slowly

## 116 THE PSYCHOLOGY OF THE CRIMINAL

at first. At the start of any new theory of knowledge there are always eager disciples whose zeal is inclined to outrun their discretion. And it would be most unfortunate if psycho-analysis were to become discredited on account of undue and unjustified claims being made for it. But there are signs that the times are changing. The legal mind is inclined to modify its former rigid standard of "responsibility". And the whole subject of the weight which should be placed upon the mental condition of an offender will soon have to be considered, and new principles will have to be laid down. When this time comes, exponents of psycho-analysis will take their place among the revisers.

In considering the bearings of mental conflict as a causation of offences, we must not forget that, as a rule, this cause does not stand alone. The conflict may be the main cause of the primary offence. But when this primary offence has been committed various other circumstances begin to bear their part. What has been termed a "criminalistic habit of mind" begins to be formed. And then, following continued misdeeds, come all the evil results of bad habit formation. Nor is this all. Social disabilities of various kinds follow, as a result of the disapproval of society. This is one of the chief difficulties in dealing with offenders. The fact that a man has been punished for an offence tends to put him at a perpetual disadvantage. This disadvantage may be an actual, concrete one in many cases. But even if this is not so, still the fact that he has been dealt with as an offender remains as a disturbing element in the man's mind. He feels that society is against him. And this emotion goes to reinforce any already existing conflict in his mind. The idea may be produced that it is hopeless for him to attempt to lead a more social life. And this idea, even when it is mistaken, may be as potent a source of evil as if it represented a real fact. So the mere bringing to the

## THE OFFENDER'S UNCONSCIOUS MIND 117

patient's consciousness of the original cause of his trouble, making him understand the nature of his mental conflict, may not always be enough. It is always essential to do this, and sometimes it may be sufficient. But in many cases much more than this is required. When criminalistic habits have been formed, means must be taken for the formation of better habits. And in many cases this task cannot be performed unless the environmental conditions are altered. It is, as a rule, useless to apply any form of treatment unless the conditions to which the patient returns after the treatment are improved. Suppose that some repressed complex has caused a man to form habits of dishonesty or of alcoholism (certain authorities hold that alcoholism is invariably the result of a repressed homo-sexual complex). We may demonstrate to the patient the existence of this repressed complex. But little good will be done if he is sent back to his former surroundings. These reflections show why it is that reformation is so much more hopeful in young than in confirmed offenders. The habit formation has not proceeded so far. We have to concentrate our efforts on the young offender. And the success of the Borstal system is due to the cases being selected, brought under its influence young, carefully investigated, trained in better habits, and, on release, supervised as far as may be possible by means of a system of organized after-care.

One reason why the process known as religious " conversion " is so helpful, as it most undoubtedly has been in many cases, is that it produces in the convert not only a changed outlook upon life and helps him to adjust himself better to reality, but it also introduces him to an entirely new set of interests, and often gives him a complete change of surroundings and of associates.

While we are engaged upon the subject of bad-habit formation, a few words may be said upon those of

## 118 THE PSYCHOLOGY OF THE CRIMINAL

idleness. No one who has had dealings with offenders can have failed to recognize how averse they are to regular continued work. This aversion is not, of course, confined to offenders. But it is extraordinarily well marked among them. The idea of regular, systematic, and perhaps monotonous work is one which they regard with absolute horror. In this connexion the influence of military service may be mentioned, for we had, at one time, constantly to consider this. Whatever may be the advantages of life in the army, it cannot but be recognized that it consists of short periods of very strenuous action, alternating with prolonged periods of idleness. Combine this with the fact that under military conditions a man's daily wants are supplied without any thought on his part, and we have a condition of affairs which is capable of demoralizing many, and which has, in fact, done so. This refers to service during the war. But peace-service in the old days had quite as bad results in many cases. Further, during the war soldiers were encouraged to think that the cessation of hostilities would result at once in the creation of a new world. And this was combined with the deliberate, and perhaps necessary, inculcation of a vast idea of their own importance. Returning to civil life, they find that their dreams of the halcyon post-war world are shattered, and that the important way in which they were regarded while in khaki is considerably lessened. Mental conflicts have been the result. And this has conduced to unrest, which is expressed in many cases in the form of delinquency, as well as in other obvious ways.

We spoke, not far back, of the evil results to a man of the feeling that the world is against him. This feeling may be originated in some cases by the idea that he is different from other men. The author has had more than one case in which this idea has been started in a patient who suffers from a severe impediment in speech,

# THE OFFENDER'S UNCONSCIOUS MIND 119

or from epilepsy. (This particular disability will be referred to more fully in the next chapter.) The result of this may be delinquency. Another case comes to mind, that of a woman whose career of dishonesty was originated by the feeling that she was not as other women because her ovaries had been removed, surgically, in earlier life. This had resulted in a repressed complex, and the case may be said to have been cured when this complex had been brought into consciousness. At any rate, up to date, no other instance of dishonesty has occurred with her. And there are very similar cases which occur at the menopause, or, at the other end of active sexual life, at puberty. The importance of both these epochs has, of course, long been recognized. And we shall have occasion to refer to the instability of puberty later on.

We must make a further analysis of the process of anti-social grudge formation. The statement made by an offender who is convicted of dishonesty that he is quite entitled to take the money or goods of those who possess more than the average may be nothing but a rationalization. But there are certain cases in which an anti-social grudge may be the cause of delinquency. The apparent injustice of life strikes all of us, to a greater or lesser degree. " I have not so much as other people have " in the way of money, of respect, etc., may be a feeling which becomes repressed, and which may then issue into consciousness in various ways. It may result in the attempt to redress this inequality by abstracting the goods of others. Or it may find activity in other directions. The dissatisfaction with the apparent inequality in nature may be felt, not so much as regards the subject himself, as in the way in which it affects others. Many of the peculiar offences committed by fanatical political adherents probably arise from this cause. Or the two points of view may be combined in the same subject. The unhappy lot of others may

# 120 THE PSYCHOLOGY OF THE CRIMINAL

arouse in a man a violent sense of indignation. This may have to be repressed. But it still exercises a most dynamic force. And this may show itself in criminal acts of various kinds. The idea of upsetting society, or of " getting even with it " in some way, lies at the root of many offences, even when they do not appear to be in any way connected with this object. It is not very uncommon to find a repressed complex of this kind. Of course, many cases of that form of insanity known as paranoia exhibit themselves in this form. We all know the paranoiac who delivers wild, impersonal harangues, who preaches anarchy, and the like. Many of these persons are made use of by designing political agitators. The boundary line between the paranoiac and the enthusiastic politician is at all times very hard to define. It is difficult for the ordinary man who leaves politics severely alone, who has to have his political passions aroused by catchy passwords and posters, and who will not even take the trouble to vote unless driven to the poll in a motor car, to realize the enthusiasm which politicians put into their work. When a man gives up a good situation and incurs disgrace among his friends in order to give his energies to some unpopular political cause, we realize that we are dealing with the abnormal. When a woman, hitherto of respectable life, commits sensational crimes with an alleged political object, we see that the boundary of insanity has been passed. But what is not so clearly seen is that such a repressed complex may break out in some quite different line of offences. And yet we may have a person who is so indignant over some real or imagined political wrong, even when this is one which does not in any way directly concern him, that his whole life is rendered miserable and he may be quite unfitted to fulfil his ordinary duties. The author has in mind the case of a woman who was so indignant about the inequality of the divorce laws that she was quite unable

## THE OFFENDER'S UNCONSCIOUS MIND 121

to adjust herself to the ordinary facts of reality. She was entirely contented with her husband. Neither he nor she ever had the remotest thought of divorce as applied to themselves. The emotion was entirely attached to the general question. It is not hard to see how such a repressed complex might issue in the form of crime.

And the author has come across another case of a similar kind. He has in mind the analysis of a man who appeared to have a grudge against the whole of Society. To anything done, whatever it was, he appeared to be instinctively opposed. He was a man of superior education, and the origin of the trouble appeared to be that, when a junior student at a well-known educational institution, he was not treated by his seniors with the respect which he believed himself to deserve. No doubt the analysis might have been carried further back still.

On Freud's theory, elements of sexuality are present from birth. Normally, the individual develops gradually until his sexuality attains its proper goal. But the process of development does not always get as far as this ; and any point on the road which this development follows may become a " point of fixation ". Instances are quite well known of girls who are unable to detach their affection from their parents. If they marry they make cold wives, and much domestic unhappiness results from this cause. Such events are not so common among men. But we do get instances of men who are never able to overcome the parental authority. In these cases the self-assertive instinct is repressed, and it may escape from the unconscious in most surprising ways. The author has had cases where this repressed instinct has got free in the form of indecent exhibitionism and of obscene language. It is always well to keep this phenomenon in mind, when one deals with such outbreaks in men of hitherto irreproachable

9

## 122 THE PSYCHOLOGY OF THE CRIMINAL

life. In some such cases, taking quite a small amount of alcohol seems to be enough to turn the scale against the inhibiting forces which have been maintaining the repressed complex in the unconscious. In all cases of a sudden outbreak occurring after a moderate amount of alcohol, it would be well to see whether psychoanalysis will not disclose some repressed mental conflict. And anger may act in just the same way. So we may conceive a man who is in a state of mental conflict. The inhibiting forces are just strong enough to retain a repressed complex in the unconscious (although it may escape in dreams). The repression involves a waste of psychic energy. But all is apparently well until there comes some sudden stress, and the balance turns against the inhibiting forces, and the repressed complex escapes with dynamic effect.

Often one may trace a delinquent career back to some experience in early childhood, some severe repression by parents, some feeling that another member of the family enjoys more consideration, and, especially, some unsatisfactory answer given to inquiries. Such deceptions on the part of parents and teachers, when recognized as deceptions, may work almost untold harm. Perhaps wrong answers to questions propounded on sex topics form the most frequent instance, because these topics are among the main problems which the childish mind grapples with.[1] The answers given by parents and teachers are known to be false or evasive far more often than the givers have any idea of. And the resulting complex may issue in " wrong doing " of a sexual nature or of some other nature. Sex complexes are not the only ones which are made to function in this way, by false or evasive answers. There are others. Such is the unity of mental life that we may have sexual or non-sexual complexes issuing in the form of sexual

[1] " A Young Girl's Diary ", translated by Eden and Cedar Paul.

# THE OFFENDER'S UNCONSCIOUS MIND 123

or non-sexual delinquencies. Reflection on the harm which is done in the way just indicated tends to produce serious thought upon the manner in which we now deal with such problems. The author has no definite proposal to put forward. And he realizes the complexity of the question. But it seems to him that it may be necessary to alter, radically, many of our ideas on this subject and to reject some of our most cherished taboos.

Into the question of sexual abnormalities the author does not intend to enter at any length. For one thing, the size of this book would not permit of the devotion of the necessary space, for the subject is of enormous dimensions. And there are other reasons. But it must not be assumed that he regards these abnormalities as unimportant. They are of the first importance. No one should attempt to adjudicate on delinquency without having made a thorough study of these subjects. That they should be of importance is not remarkable when we consider the importance of the sex-instinct. And the frequency with which one meets with instances of this kind in mental work is amazing. Students are referred to Kraft Ebings's book,[1] of which an English translation is to be had, or better still to the masterly work of Havelock Ellis,[2] a book which, to the disgrace of our country, has to be obtained from America. The author believes that nothing but good would result from the fullest and most free discussion of these subjects. They are usually condemned as loathsome, perhaps because the desire common to all of us to know more about them has been repressed into the unconscious and replaced in consciousness by its opposite. But such repressions are productive of enormous harm. A man is entitled, if he pleases, to say that these subjects are not to be studied. But he is not entitled then to declare that the results obtained from their study are

[1] " Psychopathia Sexualis."
[2] " Studies in the Psychology of Sex."

## 124 THE PSYCHOLOGY OF THE CRIMINAL

unimportant. Nearly all, perhaps all, cases of mental conflict can be traced back, ultimately, to a repressed complex of this kind. This repression exists in all of us, only in many cases its energy is sublimated into other channels. The author is writing quite seriously when he says that, in his opinion, the freedom from neurosis which characterizes the medical profession is due to the fullness with which the importance of this sex complex has been recognized from their student days, and the freedom with which the subject has been discussed by them. Conventional morality is a strange thing. Girls are (quite properly) brought up to regard marriage as being the most important duty of their lives, and yet are taught nothing whatever about its duties and responsibilities.

One point must be discussed rather more fully. Masturbation is so frequent a thing amongst delinquents that it possesses considerable importance. Probably the frequency of this habit among the average male population is much under-estimated, and the results thereof greatly exaggerated. The habit has been assailed from a variety of standpoints. And all sorts of dire results have been asserted to flow from it. The author's view is this. The act is, in itself, physically harmless (we are now speaking of masturbation after puberty). It may be physically harmful if indulged in to excess, just as the normal sexual act may be. And one does come across instances where the delinquency appears to be the result of the debilitating physical consequences of such excess. But the harm seems, usually, to arise in this way. The patient has the desire to masturbate. He also has the idea that the act is disgraceful, " morally wrong," or physically harmful. A mental conflict thus arises. One or other of the complexes is repressed. Hence may follow all the results which we have indicated as arising from such conflict and repression. And either the patient mastur-

## THE OFFENDER'S UNCONSCIOUS MIND 125

bates, and represses the idea of guilt, and the results of this may be bad. Or else he represses the sexual desire, and unless the sexual energy can be sublimated the results of this repression may be even more dire.

There is an occurrence known as " regression ", in which a man's mental condition becomes " thrown back " to some earlier stage, to childhood, or even further back than that. (Cases were found during the war in which men regressed back to an animal, a pre-human, stage of development.) May not this process be the explanation of those unfortunate, but far from infrequent, cases in which an elderly man attacks small children, or attempts in other ways to gratify his primitive instincts.

In all these and similar considerations it must always be clearly understood that the unconscious is " non-moral ". It is common to speak of unconscious impulses as " immoral ". And they are " immoral " when measured by the standard which our conscious mind now sets up. But they are not immoral in themselves. " The unconscious dates from a period preceding any knowledge of good and evil. . . . Hence the legend of the Golden Age of Innocence."[1]

Right and wrong, moral and immoral, are all terms which are transcended in the unconscious, as, according to Spinoza, they are also transcended in the " Absolute ".

We should try and realize how complicated a system our conventional civilization is. We require every person born into that society to adapt himself to it. Hints have been given as to the difficulties which accompany the process of sublimation. And yet Society wants every individual to attain to the same, and that a high degree of sublimation. We cannot be surprised that there are some failures to attain this. We have, in recent years, begun to realize that our educational system is faulty, in that it has hitherto

[1] Ernest Jones, " Papers on Psycho-analysis ", p. 633.

## 126 THE PSYCHOLOGY OF THE CRIMINAL

attempted to train every child on the same lines, and to set up a model to which every child must, if possible, be made to conform. All sorts of evils have resulted from this attempt, and we have been making tentative attempts to alter it. May we not hope that a similar reform will occur in our way of treating our delinquents. We no longer, perhaps, try to set up an absolute, cast-iron standard, as was the case with our criminal institutions in old days. But we still have a long way to go. A general objection is taken to the teaching of the new psychology. That science states that we must, in the interests of the community as well as those of the individual, evolve some social system which will give a satisfactory amount of liberty to the primary instincts as well as to the process of sublimation. And it is objected that this liberty for the instincts may have undesirable results. But the energy arising from the instincts can tend towards sublimation, as well as to the fulfilment of primitive wishes; given some reasonably satisfactory outlet for the latter, part of the available energy will tend to be sublimated. And again, we must remember that it is only by understanding what the primitive instincts are, and in what directions they tend, that we can get any control over them at all. Merely repressing the emotions which are born of these instincts has the effect of rendering them unavailable for useful purposes.

Very serious mental conflicts may be produced by doing unsuitable work. We may have a man engaged in work which he knows could easily be performed by a man of much inferior mental equipment. Conversely, we may have a man who feels that the work he does is too much for his intellectual powers. Or the work may be distasteful for other reasons. It may be hoped that the wider applications of intelligence and vocational tests will result in better vocational adjustment, and will prevent some at least of these misfits. Delinquency

## THE OFFENDER'S UNCONSCIOUS MIND 127

may be the result of such conflicts as these. And may we not also say that we can, in a somewhat similar way, have ill-adjusted ideals. A man's ideals may be above the work which he does, and vice versa.

The various " herds ", national, social, religious, and the like, into which men are collected, owe their influence and their cohesion to what may be termed social suggestibility. This lies at the very root of social life. But there is an abnormal suggestibility which has its part in producing delinquency. Individuals differ very widely in their degree of susceptibility to suggestion. And, as a rule, this susceptibility decreases as age increases, although there are not lacking instances to the contrary. We see a gradual development of the instinct of self-assertion. (In the commencement, the fœtus finds all its desires satisfied in the Nirvana of intra-uterine life, and so has no need for self-assertion.) Sometimes the instinct of self-assertion is very strongly developed from the start, and we then have a condition which is known as contra-suggestion. Some children show this for a time, and then revert to the normal. But in others the characteristic remains permanent throughout life. It may have been determined by the formation of dislike for some personal influence on account of some unwise attempt to exercise that influence. But, reverting to suggestion, it is constantly said of people that they are " easily led ", and that they will do anything they are told to do by anyone. The author is inclined to take this trait as being one meaning of the often-used expression " weakness of will ". It is common, and no doubt often correct, for offenders to attribute their downfall to the evil influence of companions.

The author does not wish to say that undue susceptibility to suggestion is more common among offenders than among non-offenders. But, as regards the former, it is certainly a point which has to be kept in mind.

## 128 THE PSYCHOLOGY OF THE CRIMINAL

Several of the tests, described in Chapter II, have been included in the series because of their tendency to bring out this important point. Of course, a person who is unduly susceptible to suggestion is so far disposed towards delinquency if he gets among people who make bad suggestions to him. (Incidentally, he should also be susceptible to the influence of good suggestions, a hopeful fact which is taken advantage of by many religious and social organizations.) The influence of the criminal " gang " has to be considered. We hear more of this in America, and the reader is referred to Healy for a full discussion of its influence.

We have cases of undue susceptibility to suggestion by one particular person, a girl to that of a man, or vice versa. In nearly all these cases psycho-analysis brings out the fact that there is some sexual bond, either an actual sexual tie, or the joint possession of some sexual secrets. This may occur among persons of the same sex. And the influence of a kind of hero-worship also occurs. Here again there is always some repressed sexual motive at work. And we have also cases in which two persons may mutually induce each other to commit some offence of which either would have been incapable alone.

Our constant references to early experiences make it clear that we must consider the environmental conditions of childhood far more than we have done in the past. Parents affect their children in other, and in more important, ways than by heredity. It has been said that nearly all the " facts " of heredity will have to be re-proved in the psychical sphere, and very many in the physical.[1] We have tended to lay undue stress on heredity in the past, and the consequences have been bad. Indeed on our delinquents themselves the effect has been almost disastrous. The ill effects of heredity have been so much impressed upon them, by all sorts of agencies, including the religious dogmas

[1] See Baudouin's " Suggestion and Auto-Suggestion ".

## THE OFFENDER'S UNCONSCIOUS MIND 129

relating to " original sin ", that a pessimistic habit of thought has been induced. " It is no use my struggling against my (delinquent) tendencies, they are in my blood," has often been said to the author by his patients. And upon society the result has been hardly less serious. We have contented ourselves with the easy " explanation " of " bad heredity ", and we have left untouched certain environmental conditions which were within our power to ameliorate, had we taken the trouble to try. We have overlooked the fact that bad heredity often implies bad environment as a direct accompaniment and consequence. Considerations of this kind show us why it is that removal from bad environment has often had such splendid results, even in the face of the worst heredity. To eliminate bad heredity, if it were possible, would be a long and a difficult process. Physical environmental conditions are more under our control, although the task in this direction is hard enough. The conditions under which children are trained are still more under our control. There is need for the education of parents in this subject, and it is one of which the study should be compulsory for all teachers.

We have seen that psycho-analysis has now a much wider scope than its original application to the cure of certain nervous diseases. We have also seen reason to hope that some cases of delinquency will be favourably affected by psycho-analysis. The beginnings of delinquency go back to early life, far further back than was at one time deemed possible. The real basic problem of delinquency is not its cure, but its prevention. These things being so, may we not make a further step ? May we not say that the place where delinquency can be prevented is in our schools and homes, and that a really good system of education would obviate much delinquency in after life ? Not only may we say this, but it is actually said. The statement has become a

## 130 THE PSYCHOLOGY OF THE CRIMINAL

truism. Surely then it follows that we must make a plea for the study of the unconscious mind by teachers, so that they may understand the tremendous effect which this has upon mental development, and so upon conduct. It is often said that the true function of a teacher is not to attempt to form the pupil's mind upon some model which is in accordance with his own wishes and ideals, but rather in accordance with those possibilities and dispositions which he may find to be inherent in the mind of the child. It is the task of the teacher to ensure that, as far as may be possible, no future harm to society, or to the child himself, shall ensue from the dispositions of the child ; that the child's tendencies are guided in useful directions ; and that there will be no future need for a process of re-education, which is, in a sense, what psycho-analysis means.

The task of the teacher and the task of the psycho-analyst are separate and distinct. It is not necessary, it is not desirable, that the teacher should practise psycho-analysis himself. It is for him, working as he does on the mind at a time when it is most susceptible to influence, to discover which of the child's tendencies are likely to obtain expression in undesirable directions, and to enable the child to divert these tendencies into other directions. If, unhappily, this is not possible, if neurotic symptoms, or bad-habit formations, or character deviations have already appeared, then it will be for the psycho-analyst to step in.

We hear much, nowadays, of preventing the beginnings of physical disease. And descriptions of, or suggestions for, prophylactic measures rightly form part of a treatise on general medicine. And since it may be said, without undue paradox, that the true object of law-makers and law-administrators should be to make laws unnecessary, the author makes no apology for introducing these few remarks upon the interest which psycho-analysis should have for the teacher, into a

## THE OFFENDER'S UNCONSCIOUS MIND 131

work dealing with the investigation of those delinquents who have come before our Courts.

This aspect of the subject shows itself to be of great importance when we remember how deleterious the effect of the general relaxation and excitement which occurred during the war, and from which few of us were able to keep ourselves free, will be upon the children who were born and were growing up during that time.

As we pursue our studies in psycho-analysis it is borne in upon us ever more and more, how essential it is that we should study our patients as individuals. We get an ever increasing insight into the complicated nature of what we call personality, and yet of how necessary it is that we should study it. This is the task of psycho-analysis on its diagnostic side. In one sense it is true that an individual, at any particular moment, consists of the " body " and the " psyche " as they exist at that moment. Yet this is but a superficial view of the matter. We should strive to envisage the individual as he really is. This, pushed to its limit, would involve a complete understanding of his whole history. We must try and think of the individual as something which has been produced by conditions which have acted since the first moment of his fœtal life. These conditions comprise :—

(1) His ancestors, immediate and remote ; (2) the conditions under which he has developed in intra-uterine life ; (3) the effects of the whole of his extra-uterine environment ; (4) reactions to all his various mental processes : and we have seen reason to think that these are perhaps the most important of all the conditions which have acted upon him. To know a man completely would involve complete knowledge of all these conditions, and this is impossible. But we must always try to learn as much as we can on each of these heads. And yet the feeling that we can know but little, hard as we may try, should surely make us modest and tolerant in our judgments of others. It is because

## 132 THE PSYCHOLOGY OF THE CRIMINAL

psycho-analysis seems likely to assist us in the understanding of what we have seen to be the direct cause of conduct, namely, mental life, that the study of this science appears to offer such hopeful prospects in the study and the treatment of delinquency.

And what is the conclusion of the matter ? Surely it is summed up in the familiar saying that " to understand all is to pardon all." The author does not mean that nothing is to be done to delinquents. He considers them to be worthy of the most careful treatment. His point is that this treatment will merely be blind unless it is based on careful individual study. This study must be complete. And it cannot be complete unless it has comprised an investigation of the unconscious mind. These principles sum up all that the author has tried to say in this chapter. All kinds of people are concerned in the treatment of offenders,— judges, magistrates, lawyers, court officials, probation workers, officers in institutions of all kinds. For all of these a full understanding of the individual offender is essential.

But it is not meant that these persons are to attempt to make the necessary investigations for themselves. The Court must have the ultimate responsibility of dealing with the case. But it must employ experts in making the investigations.

It is becoming clearer every day that it is well worth our while to have these indispensable studies of offenders fully and properly carried out.

CHAPTER V

## THE VARIOUS CLASSES OF OFFENDERS

CERTAIN classes of offenders are marked off from others by such special characteristics, and present such special problems in respect of investigation and treatment, that they require separate consideration.

1. *Mental Defectives.*—The study of the individual offender is not wholly new. We can trace its gradual growth in various directions. Society has long recognized that certain forms of mental disease cause a profound disturbance of the personality. Regarded from a certain standpoint, such forms of disease are known by the name of " insanity ". Society has adopted the position that its reaction to the conduct of persons who suffer from insanity should differ from its reaction to the conduct of other persons, although this altered reaction has taken different forms at different times and places. Further, society has seen that its reaction towards insane offenders must be defined. And the gradual development of this idea is a study of the most entrancing kind. We cannot enter into this here. Suffice it to say that people to-day would be horrified could they learn how many insane persons were hanged during (say) the eighteenth century.

Next, leaving mental disease, we have cases of the arrest of mental development. This is what is meant by mental deficiency. All who have ever studied the development of a child have recognized that its intellectual powers increase, even as its days do grow.

## 134 THE PSYCHOLOGY OF THE CRIMINAL

The infant learns to talk, to walk, and to cease to be " wet and dirty " in a more or less regular manner. And any marked retardation in the age at which an infant reaches one of these stages has been recognized as being a reason for anxiety as to the child's future on the part of the mother. This process extends beyond infancy. It has long been known that children attain a mental capacity for particular school tasks at more or less definite ages. We have heard of children of four years who were said to be capable of learning Greek, but we recognize such cases as abnormal. In certain cases this gradual mental development is arrested at a higher or lower level; the individual does not develop mentally beyond a certain level. Our recognition of this fact has been very gradual. Not so long ago, it was held that a man was either to be regarded as insane within a somewhat rigid legal definition, or was to be treated as entirely normal. As time went on, tentative attempts were made to differentiate mental defectives when they entered our penal institutions. But it was the work of Alfred Binet which first put the matter on a scientific basis. By applying tests to very large numbers of children, he demonstrated that the average child attains the power of performing certain mental operations at certain definite ages. We thus saw our way to obtaining standards by which mental defect could be detected and, to some extent, measured.

The report of the Royal Commission on the Feeble-minded did much to clarify our views, and to sketch out the nature of possible methods of dealing with defectives. It also showed how great were the divergencies between the estimates made by different observers as to the numbers of the defective class, these divergencies being largely due to lack of precision in definition. And it provided us with a tentative definition. Next, the passing of the Mental Deficiency Act, 1913, made it possible to deal legally with defectives.

## VARIOUS CLASSES OF OFFENDERS 135

And, from our present point of view, the most important provisions are those which endeavour to prevent defectives from becoming inmates of our penal institutions, and to remove them therefrom if they find their way there. The passage of this Act was attended with violent opposition in certain quarters, and the working of the Act is still hindered, in some places, by indifference and even by open hostility.

The question at once arises, Are we to take a certain " mental age ", as arrived at by the Binet or some other scale, as an unyielding standard for the diagnosis of mental defect ? By some enthusiasts this question is answered in the affirmative. And the American Association for the study of the Feeble-minded has laid down the following classification. (It must be remembered that in America the term " feeble-minded " is employed as a general description of the mentally defective class, and not, as with us, for one particular sub-division of that class. In America the term " moron " more or less corresponds with the term " feeble-minded " as used in this country) . . . . " Idiots," on this classification, " are those who are able to perform the mental tests up to the level of the normal child of 2 years. Imbeciles are those able to do the tests up to 7 years. And morons are those able to do the tests up to 12 years."

With idiots we are not concerned in Court work, and we need give no further time to them. Imbeciles are occasionally met with. The author found twelve imbeciles (and three other doubtful cases of imbecility) among 6,615 consecutive cases received into Birmingham Prison. But the recognition of imbeciles is easy, and we need not discuss them further. They seldom come under notice in Court work, probably because they are recognized early, and, in most communities, are quickly dealt with. It is with the feeble-minded, using the term in the English sense, and especially with the higher

## 136 THE PSYCHOLOGY OF THE CRIMINAL

grades thereof, that the difficulty begins. So far as the " mental age " of 9 years, or under that standard, there is but little uncertainty. If an individual definitely grades below that age there is strong ground for saying that he requires permanent care. It is of interest that the U.S. Army found it to be of little use retaining men of a " mental age " below 9 years in the ranks. But above that standard all is uncertain. It must be remembered that, in Court work, we are not grading people from the point of view of scientific information. A definite suggestion as to treatment has to be made, or should be made. And very serious results may follow on calling a person mentally defective. The Royal Commission defined feeble-minded persons as those " who were capable of earning a living under favourable circumstances, but were incapable, from mental defect existing from birth or from an early age, of (a) *managing themselves or their affairs with ordinary prudence, or (b) of competing on equal terms with their normal fellows.*" The Mental Deficiency Act defines them as persons " who by reason of mental defectiveness existing from birth or from an early age [1] *require care, supervision, and control, for their own protection or the protection of others.*" Both definitions contain the proviso that the mental defect must have existed from an early age, thus excluding such cases of weak mentality as may supervene in later life. The author was at one time of opinion that these words were a bar to the full usefulness of the Act. But he has seen reason to change this view. We certainly have cases of early senile dementia which cannot perhaps be certified as amounting to definite " insanity ", and which are the cause of delinquency. And the author is also of opinion that there is a definite type of what may be called " alcoholic " feeble-mindedness, produced by the prolonged action of alcohol upon a previously normal person, although in the majority of

[1] The words " early age " are defined by the Amending Act, 1927, as meaning before the age of 18 years.

## VARIOUS CLASSES OF OFFENDERS 137

cases it is a mental defect which has occasioned the alcoholism. This alcoholic type of feeble-mindedness is, perhaps, a temporary matter, and may be curable by abstention from alcohol, although the evidence at present available on this point is inconclusive. The senile type is, of course, permanent, and may progress (as may also the alcoholic type) to definite, certifiable " insanity ". It would seem that these types of mental defect require legislation, but that this should be distinct from that connected with the defective class now dealt with by the Act.

But it is the italicized words in the two definitions that are of importance. Before a person can be dealt with under the Act we have to prove (*inter alia*) that he requires care, supervision, and control, for his own protection or for that of others. And we may fairly read this in conjunction with the Royal Commission's definition. The person must be shown to be incapable of competing on equal terms with his normal fellows (meaning, presumably, his equals in education, social position, etc.), or of managing himself and his affairs with ordinary prudence (including, presumably, the making of those social adjustments which all who aspire to ordinary existence in the world have to make). If a person cannot do these things by reason of mental defect and if, by reason of this mental defect, he constantly falls into delinquency, then it is clear that he requires care, supervision, and control, for his own protection and for that of others. The author does not believe that the mere failure to attain any particular standard of " mental age " is, *per se*, enough to bring a person under this heading. We do not know what the grading of many of the lower classes of our daily labourers would be ; there is a great field open for work in this direction. But it seems very probable that many persons who would be quite unable to do the twelve-year tests and some at least of the ten-year tests, are

## 138 THE PSYCHOLOGY OF THE CRIMINAL

yet doing quite useful work in the world, are good citizens, and never fall into delinquency. The whole history of each case has to be considered. On the other hand, good reason will often be found for the segregation of cases which grade at ten years, and for some which grade nearly up to 12 years. Of course, higher-grade cases are much more trainable than are the lower-grade cases. Many can be trained in good habits of industry, etc., if taken in hand early enough. And this training is of much practical importance.

If a case grades at 12 years, or higher, and we are quite certain that we are not dealing with a " verbalist " (a term which will be explained later) then it is doubtful if we have any right to describe it as one of mental defect.

Every mental defective is at least a potential delinquent. Why do defectives tend so strongly to fall into delinquency ? Terman[1] answers the question thus : he says, " Morality depends upon (a) Ability to foresee and weigh possible consequences for ourselves and others of different kinds of behaviour, and (b) Willingness and capacity to exercise self-restraint. There are many intelligent criminals because (a) may exist without (b). But (b) presupposes (a). Moral judgment, like business judgment, or any other form of higher thought process, is a function of intelligence." Thus Terman, like the present author, would seem to reject the idea of a " moral sense " as apart from the intelligence.

Defect of intelligence has always a tendency to lead to anti-social conduct. As a rule, the greater is a man's intelligence, the more he realizes the importance and the claims of the community, although he may, in some cases, look past the surrounding community, towards a greater community, perhaps one as yet unborn. This has always been so. The greatest minds of antiquity

[1] " The Measurement of Intelligence."

## VARIOUS CLASSES OF OFFENDERS 139

recognized this. In the Middle Ages it was the intelligent part of Society which grasped at the chance of the best community life then known. And it was this feeling which elaborated the ideal of the Catholic Church. It is so to-day. Our intelligence, as well as our emotional feeling, is tending from individualism, towards a more collective type of Society.

A word may be said as to the causes of mental defect. There is no doubt that the main cause is bad heredity. Inquiries have amply justified this statement. And this is, of course, one great reason for the control of these cases. We can in this way, and it is the only practicable way, prevent a new generation of defectives (who would have their defect accentuated) from being a burden to our successors. Parental alcoholism has also been assigned as a cause. There is much reason to doubt the truth of this. For (1) Alcoholism is a very prevalent condition ; (2) we have no statistics as to the incidence of alcoholism in the parents of normal children ; (3) we have no reliable statistics of the proportion of normal to defective children among alcoholic parents ; (4) alcoholism is only a symptom of some unstable mental condition. So that abnormal characteristics in the children of alcoholic parents are very likely to be due to the effect of the inheritance of this unstable mental condition.

In considering the success, or alleged success, of a defective in earning a living, we have to consider the kind of work which he does, the supervision given to him, and the competition which he has to face. Many defectives appear to have done fairly well in the Army. A number of them never got further than the base. But employed on simple tasks, with constant supervision, with all their daily wants supplied without thought on their part, and with no competition to face, the life was just what many of them wanted. It is, more or less, what the life in a good institution for such

## 140 THE PSYCHOLOGY OF THE CRIMINAL

cases means. It is surely possible for us to arrange something on these lines, even when the war is over. Our care for our defectives need not cease when they are no longer in khaki.

It must always be remembered that no defective adult can be dealt with under the Act unless he is found guilty of an offence, or is found to be neglected, or under certain other conditions.

Mental defect is not the same thing as backwardness, although a mental defective is backward. Tredgold[1] takes the view that the characteristic which differentiates the defective from the merely dull is the absence of " common sense ". The author ventures to think that several of the tests in his scheme are useful in ascertaining the presence or absence of this particular quality.

There is a type of defective, described by Healy, and called by him the " verbalist " type. The special characteristic of members of this class is their great ability in the use of language, and this fact is of considerable practical importance. These cases are very likely to grade high on the Binet scale. For this scale, and its modification by Terman, is very favourable to the subject who possesses language ability. This is one reason for dissatisfaction with the Terman scale. On account of his facility in the use of language the verbalist may be able to deal with many situations without any suspicion arising as to his being a mental defective. And it may be difficult to persuade some persons that a subject who can talk very fluently is really a mental defective. Such a subject is likely to mislead even the examiner. And this is why the author so strongly urges the use of some other scheme of tests in addition to, or instead of, the Terman scale. If the subject grades high on the Terman scale, but fails to make a respectable show on tests of a " performance "

[1] " Mental Deficiency."

## VARIOUS CLASSES OF OFFENDERS 141

character, then the question as to whether we are not dealing with a verbalist must be considered. As a result of their mental defect, these persons are always mentally unbalanced. And their ability in the use of language is very likely to lead them into all sorts of troublesome situations, often causing them to be untruthful and fraudulent. Such cases are, of course, only particular examples of mental defectives who have some special ability.

On the other hand, we have a type of case which may appear to be mentally defective, on account of having poor language ability. Such cases are fairly familiar in ordinary life. A case of this kind may grade low on the Terman scale. But if the subject makes a good show on " performance " tests, the author would not regard him as mentally defective. Delinquents usually come from a class in which verbal fluency is not marked ; they have little practice in verbal expression. We recognize in daily life that there is a marked distinction between glib superficiality and real capacity which expresses itself badly in words. But the precise differentiation between the two conditions may be very difficult.

2. *Special Abilities and Special Disabilities.*—No one can work for any length of time among offenders without coming to the conclusion that many defectives show very remarkable variations. We may find that a subject may be markedly defective and yet may show some special ability. Such marked instances as that of the " Earlswood genius " described by Tredgold[1] are not often found. But in a lesser degree we frequently find, as a result of routine testing, an individual who, although he is defective, yet does well in some particular line of tests. For example, we may find hopeless failure on all tests except those which involve routine memory, or on those which involve the handling

[1] " Mental Deficiency."

## 142 THE PSYCHOLOGY OF THE CRIMINAL

of concrete material such as the form boards. When this is found, it is clear that we are dealing with a defective who has some special ability. And it is hardly necessary to point out how important this may be in respect of the advice to be given as regards treatment, e.g. what particular institution such a case should be remitted to. In the same way we get cases which are not defectives, and yet have some particular disability. A word of caution is needed here. For in cases of epilepsy and hysteria we may get results which can be confused with those of special disability.

Many situations in life do not require any marked mental ability for the due performance of their duties. There are defectives who have some amount of insight into their own disability, and who are prepared to content themselves with lowly forms of labour. This has to be remembered. For in Court work we, of course, only see the failures, those who have not been able to meet Society's views as to conduct. But there can be no doubt that there are many defectives who are " carrying on " quite well in a lowly sphere. And this must put us on our guard against the danger of deciding on the results of tests alone. Conduct and other matters have also to be considered. This is one reason for the application of well-devized systems of group tests to large bodies of persons in various stations of life.

3. *Subnormal Offenders.*—Among our delinquents we find that there is a well-marked group the members of which are not definite mental defectives, and yet are not normal mentally. We are not now speaking of mental defectives in whom there is a difficulty in proving the existence of defect from an early age. It is not easy to frame a term for the class which we are now considering. Healy has suggested the term " subnormal ". The author has found this term convenient, and he proposes to use it. There are obvious objections, for mental defectives are subnormal. But, on the whole,

## VARIOUS CLASSES OF OFFENDERS 143

the term seems as free from objection as any other. (Some writers have used the term " weak-minded " for all cases which show mental abnormality, whether certifiable under the Act or not.) There is sometimes a doubt in the examiner's mind as to whether any particular case should be regarded as a mental defective. When this doubt exists, it is the author's invariable custom to place the case in this subnormal class ; the result of certification as a mental defective being far-reaching and serious. Of course, a report can be made to the Court, pointing out the subject's mental condition, and suggesting appropriate disposal. In some cases we may say that a man is so defective that he is certain to be constantly getting into trouble, if allowed to be at large. But in every doubtful case we have to weigh all the factors, and not that of intelligence alone. Again, in other cases there may be apparent mental defect, and yet we may not feel certain whether this defect is not a temporary condition, perhaps due to some physical cause. On a few occasions the author has had an opportunity of re-examining cases of this kind, and has found that the apparent mental defect has disappeared.

In all these cases the standard with which the individual is compared has to be considered. Take the case of a boy who is born and brought up among people of considerable intellectual capacity. Such a boy may be regarded as subnormal by his family. And, compared with their standard, he is so. Whereas, judged by some lower standard, he might be considered normal. In such a case as that just instanced the feeling of inferiority may produce a mental conflict, and delinquency may result from this cause.

4. *Epileptics.* The connexion between epilepsy and delinquency has long been noted. Lombroso's view was that the criminal is, essentially, an epileptic. This view is no longer maintained. But, although it

## 144 THE PSYCHOLOGY OF THE CRIMINAL

may not be acceptable literally, there is no doubt that it is very tempting. For features which characterize the epileptic are found in many delinquents. We have, in both cases, the outbreaks of ill-temper and violence, without any apparent provocation, the pecular variations in temperament, and the fact that these characteristics present a certain periodicity. To these may be added the egocentric nature of both classes, their lack of emotional control, and even their marked tendency to religiosity. Yet there are difficulties which must be duly weighed. Epilepsy is stated to be about as common among women as among men. And yet, in the author's experience, epileptic attacks are comparatively uncommon among female offenders, although it is only fair to say that this experience has chiefly lain among male offenders. Although he has no precise figures, the author has a distinct impression that epilepsy is decidedly less common in prisons now than was the case twenty years ago. Perhaps this decrease, if real, may be due to more careful segregation of the marked cases. Among Healy's series of 1,000 consecutive cases there were, including both definite and doubtful case, 8·5 per cent of epileptics.

A lengthy description of epilepsy would be out of place. But a few words must be said. The characteristics of the classical or " major " convulsion are well known. " Minor " epileptic attacks (*petit mal*) take the form of a momentary loss of consciousness, or of some muscular spasm of brief duration. But there are also two kinds of phenomena which have very important legal bearings.

(1) *Post-epileptic automatism*. This often occurs after a minor attack. The patient may perform some action which appears to be purposive. For example, he may undress in the street ; and many other varieties of such conduct are recorded.

(2) *Epileptic Equivalents*. In these, automatic states

## VARIOUS CLASSES OF OFFENDERS 145

occur in place of the convulsion. They vary greatly in their duration. And different mental conditions may occur ; depression, excitement, confusion, etc. The conduct during these equivalents may be apparently normal, so that abnormality may not be suspected. Or criminal actions may be performed. After the attack is over, there is usually complete loss of memory for the actions performed during the attack, but this rule is not absolute.

Criminal actions performed during these equivalents may give rise to much difficulty in Court work. A Court is, naturally, sometimes reluctant to accept this explanation of an offence. All the circumstances must be weighed. Evidence as to other epileptic manifestations is of much importance. An outbreak of sudden, perhaps of apparently motiveless violence is very suggestive, especially if there was no attempt at concealment.

The epileptic presents several other characteristics which are of interest to those who work among offenders.

(*a*) There is a peculiar intellectual variability. With the series of mental tests described in Chapter II, the author has often been struck by the very " mixed " display of results given by epileptics. We may have brilliant and rapid success on some tests, together with utter failure or very slow performance on others. There may be marked variations in the results obtained from tests of the same kind. When we scan a set of test results, in which this variation is shown, consideration should always be given to the possibility of epilepsy. Or we may have marked differences, not accountable for in other ways, in the test results obtained on two different days. The peculiar variations in mood and temper among epileptics are well known. Attacks of ill-temper may precede or may follow the typical fit, or they may in some cases replace this manifestation (this being one form of epileptic equivalent).

(*b*) There is a marked tendency to self-esteem and to

# 146 THE PSYCHOLOGY OF THE CRIMINAL

egotistic feelings generally. This leads to self-assertion. Impulsiveness is often well marked. Then there are sometimes strong sexual impulses, due to the exaggeration of the egocentric feelings. Stoddart [1] expresses the view that the primary factors in epilepsy are purely mental in origin. During an epileptic equivalent the patient's conscious mind is in abeyance, and the unconscious mind holds the field. This no doubt accounts for the sexual offences, sometimes of a perverted character, which are so common in these states. The epileptic character is essentially childish. This is illustrated in many ways, some of which have just been indicated. Further, we have the evidence given by the word association tests, in which the reactions made by epileptics closely resemble those of children and imbeciles.

(c) There is a general and gradual deterioration in the mental powers.

The statement has been made that in epilepsy there is a defect of the " moral sense ". What happens is that there is some intellectual failure, combined with marked exaggeration of the egocentric feelings.

We see, from all the above considerations, why it is that the epileptic shows such marked tendencies to delinquency. But other factors come into play. (1) The feeling that he is not as other men are, and the anti-social grudge produced thereby. (2) Constant loss of places of work and failure to obtain work on account of the disease. Hence arises the formation of bad and anti-social habits. Epileptics specially require training in self-control and in good habits. On the whole, epileptics present as difficult problems as any with which Courts have to deal.

5. *Psychopaths.* There exists a class of persons who are not " insane " and not mentally defective in the sense of being certifiable as such. Further, they

---

[1] " Mind and its Disorders ", Third Edition, p. 401.

## VARIOUS CLASSES OF OFFENDERS 147

cannot be grouped among the epileptics or the psycho-neurotics. But their mental condition is such that they are unable to make proper adjustments to the demands of Society. We dealt in some measure with this group in the last chapter, regarding them from the psycho-analytic point of view. But they are of considerable importance from a court point of view. And so they merit further consideration here. The group is of a very mixed character, and it is not easy to settle on any satisfactory classification. We have practically no form of classification of them in this country. So the author proposes to adopt the classification suggested by the Surgeon-General of the United States Army.[1] Among all the recruits examined for that army there were found to be 0·55 per 1,000 rejected under this heading, and a number of other cases came to light during the training. A considerably larger percentage will be found among offenders, because these psychopaths are of such a character that they tend readily to fall into delinquency. It must be remembered that the various sub-divisions given in the adopted classification are far from being definite, and many cases present the characteristics of more than one sub-division.

(1) *Inadequate personality.* These are persons who have often had quite good social and educational advantages, but in spite of these advantages they make a complete failure of all that they undertake. This failure may arise through defect of ambition, perseverance, initiative, or judgment. And so it may be said to arise from mental defect. Many cases which are loosely spoken of as " moral imbeciles " belong to this class. But the intelligence may not be markedly affected, and they are not certifiable as defectives. Often the mental disability does not appear until the affected individual leaves the control of home and

[1] See Rosanoff, " Manual of Psychiatry ", pp. 215–28.

## 148 THE PSYCHOLOGY OF THE CRIMINAL

school, and has to face the stress of ordinary life. Every reader will be able to recall instances in his own experience. Such cases are quite common among offenders.

(2) *Paranoid Personality.* This is, really, only a lesser degree of the form of insanity known as " paranoia ", in which the patient suffers from systematized delusions. Marked development of the self-assertive instinct, combined with conceit, lies at the basis of these conditions. But, in the class which we are now considering, these characteristics do not progress to the extent of forming a delusional system. Such cases are not very often met with among offenders. But we do meet with them in those who get into difficulties with the law on what may be termed " semi-political " grounds. They are very difficult to deal with, for the practical reason that the opinions of Society, as to what degree of deviation from generally accepted conduct may be permitted on " political " grounds, are in a very fluid state. These persons present argumentativeness and fixed adherence to one particular idea, combined with distortion of values and with much contempt for the views of others.

There is a class of persons who possess very marked individuality, and who strongly resent every form of restraint and convention. These must not be confused with the paranoid psychopath class. The persons of whom we are now speaking are often full of vigour and possess much initiative. In some of these cases psychoanalysis discloses a strong complex of opposition to the father or to his representative.

(3) *Emotional Instability.* It is doubtful how far this should be admitted as a separate sub-division. Marked variability of the emotions is characteristic of most of the persons of whom we have spoken in this volume. Still such cases are of interest, because we see much of this characteristic in prison life. How far, if at all,

## VARIOUS CLASSES OF OFFENDERS 149

this is due to prison conditions, apart from the mental disposition of the subject, is a question which cannot be entered into here.

(4) *Criminalism.* This heading is placed in the Surgeon-General's list. But the author is unable to accept it. The only meaning it can have is simply habitual delinquency.

(5) *Pathological Lying.* This group has been exhaustively dealt with by W. and M. T. Healy.[1] The members of this group are of considerable practical interest, and may cause much trouble. They give no grounds for describing them as mentally defective or as insane, although the tales which they sometimes tell may at first give rise to doubts as to sanity, so amazing are they. One man persisted in the story that he had been kidnapped by four masked men, and carried off to London in a motor car, shut up in a box. It is probable that psycho-analysis would always reveal some buried complex in such cases. We must try to discover the motives for the lying, for these must be understood if we would comprehend the case. Children, especially, may actually believe in their dreamed adventures.

(6) *Sexual Psychopathy.* We may have anomalies of degree in either direction. And we may have anomalies of nature, perversion and inversion, the latter being a contrast between the physical and the psychical sex in the individual. The author has already indicated his intention not to discuss these matters in detail. But all who deal with offenders should study this subject carefully. In these cases psycho-analysis is always specially worthy of a trial.

(7) *Nomadism.* The wandering instinct is, to some extent, present in all of us. It may be a survival of some previous racial state. We are not now speaking of temporary attacks of the wandering desire (known as " fugues ") such as we may have in epilepsy, but of

[1] " Pathological Lying, Accusation, and Swindling."

## 150 THE PSYCHOLOGY OF THE CRIMINAL

the " tramp " class. Great numbers of these were met with in prison in pre-war days. During the war they almost disappeared. A few are now coming into notice again. These people will do no work unless they are obliged, and they get into trouble for trespass, larceny, and arson. Often bad sex practices, including homosexuality, occur in them. Truancy in youth is another example of this tendency, and this is often found as a basis when inquiring into the history of some offender, especially in the case of boys.

6. *Constitutional Inferiors.* There are certain cases which cannot be placed in the groups of the insane, the mentally defective, or the neurotics, but are yet of importance from our present point of view. It is not easy to devise a suitable name, but perhaps Meyer's term of constitutional inferiors is the best. They are not insane, although many of them eventually become so. But their psychical peculiarities unfit them for normal life. There may be some defect of intelligence, but often they are quite good in this respect. They are unbalanced, and their power of inhibition is lessened. They are unduly susceptible to the influence of suggestion. Their conduct is impulsive and variable. Many are marked by a special desire for alcohol. The treatment of this type has hitherto been most hopeless. They are, as a rule, well behaved in prison, but they drift into crime again as soon as they are discharged. Indefinite segregation has been suggested. It would have, in most cases, to be permanent. And the number of institutions which would be required is a bar to this proposal. It is quite possible that some sexual conflict is often at the root of the trouble in these cases.

7. *Offences at Puberty and in Adolescence.* That marked mental changes are normal at the onset of puberty requires no demonstration. In normal cases we have increase of self-control and of reasoning power,

## VARIOUS CLASSES OF OFFENDERS 151

and we get the development of ambition and of other ideals. All these, normally, act as inhibiting agents to the forces of self-assertion. But the inhibiting forces may not be strong enough, or they may not develop soon enough. And, in cases which are predisposed to mental aberration, the onset of puberty may cause an accentuation of this predisposition. As a rule, these cases ultimately develop the power of adjustment to reality. But before this adjustment takes place there may be much trouble. In the study of these cases care must be taken to distinguish those who are mentally defective from those which show merely exaggerated symptoms of the instability normal at puberty.

The treatment of such cases, where physical or mental defect is not a bar, must be mainly institutional. Many of the cases now sent to Borstal Institutions are of this type. Under the influences brought to bear at these establishments there is no doubt that many of the cases are rehabilitated. Probably in these cases the mental conflict has been solved. But the author feels strongly that we should not be content unless we try what psycho-analysis can do. He believes that in many of these cases the patient's comprehension of the nature of the mental conflict would make his " reformation " more certain and more lasting. Mental defectives can, of course, only be permanently cared for in suitable institutions.

That new situations, in the body and in the mind, occur at the time of puberty has been recognized by religious organizations, many of which have arranged special observances for that period, akin to the Anglican rite of Confirmation. There is a change from childish to adult characteristics. New impulses arise, or, rather, there is a change in the mode of expression of the primitive impulses. Marro has said that this time of life is one of " psychic hyperæsthesia ". Desires for and opportunities of new experiences arise. There is usually

## 152 THE PSYCHOLOGY OF THE CRIMINAL

a tendency to rebellion against former authority. All this makes an inclination to delinquency likely at this period. And, as a fact, the examination of the records of offenders shows that in a vast number of instances the delinquent career begins at just this time. The special form of delinquency which is probable is, as we should expect, that of impulsive misconduct. All who have studied young offenders, and listened to their life-histories, will have heard many tales which bear out this point. Often the impulses which led to some offence are very vaguely remembered. Whether these offenders are to be treated as fully " responsible " is a matter for our law-makers to decide. But of one thing we may be quite certain. The punishment of these persons as if they had been adults was productive of the most dire results. It was the recognition of this awful failure which led to (1) the establishment of the Borstal System, and (2) the Probation Act. Both of these agencies have been useful in their way. But the author feels that a great chance is being missed by not combining the benefits of psycho-analysis with both remedial plans in suitable cases. The real trouble with many of these offenders is that they do not understand why it is that they have failed to make normal adjustments. Knowledge of self, useful to all, is absolutely necessary to these persons.

With regard to Probation it may be said that it often fails because the environment has been left unaltered. The individual is left to struggle on against the drawbacks of his environment, which drawbacks may have been responsible, in a secondary way, for his delinquency. The efforts of the most admirable Probation Officer are sometimes thwarted in this way. It is often most highly desirable to remove an offender from his home surroundings.[1]

8. *Moral Insanity and Moral Imbecility.* A vast amount has been written on these two heads. The

[1] See final paragraph on page 158.

## VARIOUS CLASSES OF OFFENDERS 153

term " moral insanity " was first used by Prichard in 1835. At the present time we hear more often of " moral imbecility ". Almost every writer who has attacked these subjects has used the words in a different sense. But it appears that these differences are really fundamental, and are not due to the loose use of terms. The Mental Deficiency Act, 1913, contained a definition of " moral imbeciles." The Amending Act, 1927, has substituted the term " moral defectives," which it defines as meaning " persons in whose case there exists mental defectiveness coupled with strongly vicious or criminal propensities, and who require care, supervision, and control for the protection of others." The mental defectiveness must have existed prior to the age of 18 years). Now many habitual criminals might be brought within this definition, but for the requirement of proof of the existence of some mental defectiveness. And it may be held that we should adopt the position that habitual delinquency is, *per se*, a proof of permanent mental defect. But the time has not yet come for the complete acceptance of this position. So we are faced by the question, What kind of mental defect, as distinct from that mentioned in the definition of the " feeble-minded," is here meant ? And we come at once to the further question, Is there such a thing as a " moral sense," apart from the intellect ? The author has already stated his view that there is no such sense. What we call our " moral sense ", our ideas of " right and wrong ", seems to him to be indissolubly bound up with our social judgments, and with the gradual growth of our social relationships. Intelligence and experience (which depends upon intelligence) enter into the problem. And it really comes to this : If a man believes in the existence of some entity, call it " conscience " or " will " or any other name, which sits in judgment on our desires, and which finally decides how we should act, having in view some " absolute " standard

## 154 THE PSYCHOLOGY OF THE CRIMINAL

of right and wrong, then it is open to that man to believe in a " moral sense " and in " moral imbecility (or deficiency "). But, if we hold the doctrine of psychical determinism, then this position is quite untenable.

Many cases have arisen in which moral imbecility (or deficiency) has been advanced as a solution. But, upon investigation, they have all been found to be insane, or to be intellectually defective, or to be the subjects of some mental conflict. It is possible that some cases have been certified as " moral imbeciles (or defectives)" when there has not been enough evidence to certify them as " feeble-minded ", and yet it has been desired, for one reason or another, to have them certified.

Stephen[1] lays great stress on the question of "self-control ". He says that the man who exercises self-control refers to distant motives and general principles of conduct. Mercier[2] says that Stephen has transferred a moral principle to the domain of the intellect. Mercier says that self-control means, " the power of forgoing immediate pleasure for the sake of greater advantage in the future ". And he says that this is not a matter of the intellect, but is a moral quality. But is this so ? The power of forgoing present gratification for the sake of future advantage depends partly on memory (of what we have experienced before, have seen, heard, read, etc.), partly on judgment (which depends on memory, for judgment unites things which are already in consciousness), and partly on reason (which is the power of drawing an inference from two judgments already present, and so depends upon judgment, and so, ultimately, upon memory). And memory is surely a matter of the intellect. When memory fails, judgment and reasoning power also fail, and so self-control fails. We constantly see examples of this process.

Mercier gives as a typical instance of moral imbecility the case of the Afghan thief whose hands had been

[1] op. cit.  [2] " Criminal Responsibility."

## VARIOUS CLASSES OF OFFENDERS 155

struck off as a punishment for stealing, who had been threatened with immediate execution if he stole again, and who at once purloined an article of trivial value. If these facts, 'as given by Mercier, do not indicate defect or aberration of the intellect, then, as Healy says, we may be permitted to ask what facts would be sufficient to indicate such defect or aberration.

Most writers come, in the end, to the statement that all moral imbeciles (or defectives) are primarily abnormal intellectually. And it would be well if the terms " moral insanity " and " moral imbecility (or deficiency)" were both dropped, as tending only to confuse the issues.

The only thing which may, perhaps, be said in favour of the retention of the term " moral imbecility (or deficiency)" is that there are certain persons whose judgment appears to be defective, in that they seem unable to realize that a certain amount of deference must be paid to the society in which they happen to live. They are not quite on a par with the habitual criminal who steals because he prefers to do that rather than to work. If the latter has his particular wants supplied without thought on his part, then he may live a social life (as many of them did in the army). Whereas the former always seems to be at war with Society. If such persons are found to have a mental defect, then they are obviously cases for detention in some suitable institution. And as regards those who, without discoverable mental defect, cannot, by other means, be made to fit in with Society, there is a growing feeling that, in justice both to the offender and to itself, Society must arrange for their permanent detention in some suitable environment.

9. *Alcoholism and Other Toxic Conditions*. The connexion between alcoholism and delinquency has been most exhaustively discussed, and volumes of statistics have been produced on this topic. But the conclusions have never been wholly satisfactory. It is the old

## 156 THE PSYCHOLOGY OF THE CRIMINAL

story of truth having been sought with a view to the confirmation of some preconceived opinion.

There is, of course, no doubt at all that the prohibition or the limitation of the supply of alcoholic liquors will result in a diminution of those offences which are directly due to alcohol, and also of such offences as common assault. Incidentally it may be mentioned that prohibition would probably cause a diminution in the incidence of venereal diseases. These facts seem to have been established by our experience of the Liquor Control Regulations, although this must be discounted because of the very abnormal conditions then prevailing in other respects. Whether the diminution noted in the other forms of offences is due to the control of the supply of alcohol is another, and a much more difficult, question.

We really have to face this problem : Why is it that certain persons become alcoholics, and others do not ? Neither habitual use, nor ease of access, nor heredity, nor bad environment, seem to be enough in themselves. Clearly there are other factors at work. Mental defect has been suggested. And there is no doubt that many alcoholics are mental defectives or psycopaths. But it is not clearly proved that there is a larger proportion of alcoholics among the mental defective than among the non-defective class. And the real truth seems to be that there is a mental conflict at the root of the trouble in these cases. (Some have asserted that this conflict is, in all cases, of a homo-sexual character. Perhaps it may represent a state of " fixation ".)

In all alcoholic cases the first thing to be done is to discover whether there is mental defect. If this exists, and if it is of such a nature as to be legally certifiable, then the position is clear. An alcoholic mental defective must be permanently treated as a defective. All other forms of attempted treatment, whether by Inebriate Homes or otherwise, are obviously futile in such cases.

## VARIOUS CLASSES OF OFFENDERS 157

But if there is no certifiable mental defect then psycho-analysis should be tried. This has marked limitations. There must be a desire on the part of the patient to be cured, and he must be ready to co-operate in the treatment. Unless these conditions exist, all attempts at psycho-analysis are waste of time. Homes, in which general treatment could be combined with psycho-analysis, seem to be indicated. But the psycho-analyst must not be expected to act as superintendent as well.

Other Toxic Agencies : morphinism and cocainism are reported to be causes of delinquency, especially in the United States of America. And it would seem likely that this should be the case, when we consider the general mental degeneration which may arise from the abuse of these drugs, and the remarkable mental vagaries which may ensue. The use of these drugs is said to have much increased of late years in this country. But the author has seen very few instances of victims of either of these drugs in his work. Perhaps experience in other towns may be different, but in Birmingham such cases are certainly infrequent. There should be no great difficulty in diagnosing them under conditions in which a supply of the drug is quite unobtainable (as in prison), for the " abstinence symptoms " which result from deprivation in an *habitué* are quite unmistakable. The author has had a few men and women under his care who have told lurid tales of their drug addictions, and have endeavoured to account in this way for their delinquency. But, on testing these stories, very few were found to be even possibly credible. Marks of old hypodermic punctures are not, in the author's experience, at all common among offenders.

Tobacco. It has been stated that abuse of tobacco causes delinquency by creating instability of the nervous system. It is possible that this may occur. But the author has hardly ever found a case in which

## 158 THE PSYCHOLOGY OF THE CRIMINAL

he felt certain that tobacco was at the root of the trouble. No doubt many offenders are excessive smokers, but this is found among non-delinquents also. And it is not uncommon to hear offenders declare (and there is no apparent reason to doubt their statements in this respect) that they never smoke at all. Since the younger offenders are almost entirely cigarette smokers, the cynical might say that tobacco did not enter into the matter to any great extent.

In all these cases of the use of stimulants and sedatives, to say that they are causes of delinquency is a very superficial view to adopt. Their abuse is always a sign of some underlying mental condition, some mental conflict. This conflict is the real cause of the delinquency, as it is of the alcoholism or the drug addiction.

To place an offender upon probation is so easy and apparently so excellent a procedure that it is often resorted to without due consideration of the mentality of the person so dealt with. It is as necessary to examine an offender before placing him upon probation as before sending him to prison. An intelligent probation officer cannot fail to be assisted by an expert's report. In some cases arrangements can be made by which some form of psycho-therapy may be combined with and made a condition of probation.

## CHAPTER VI

## CONCLUSIONS

WE have considered the nature of "crime", and the character of the reaction of Society towards crime, which reaction has hitherto mainly taken the form of "punishment". Crime, in the sense of some injury inflicted upon the public, it seems likely that we shall have always with us. This being so, it is certain that Society will always react against it. A Society which expressed no reaction against those who transgressed its laws would be dead. A Society whose reaction is ineffective is growing old and decaying, and so is about to vanish away. The history of penal reform may appear as an apparently incongruous tangle of unconnected movements. But a thread runs through them all. There has been an attempt to solve the problem as to what should be the reaction of society towards crime.

It is not, however, necessary that this reaction of Society should forever take the form known as "punishment". The desirability of some change has long been recognized. And this book will have been written quite in vain if the author has not impressed upon his readers this one moral—not punishment, but *treatment*.

It has been said that every country has the government which it deserves to have. It is also true, as Lacassagne has said, that every community has the criminals which it deserves to have. And Devon[1] has put it concisely in these words: "There is only one

[1] "The Criminal and the Community."

159

## 160 THE PSYCHOLOGY OF THE CRIMINAL

principle in penology that is worth any attention ; it is to find out why a man does wrong and make it not worth his while." To find out why a man does wrong is the only true solution of the problem of delinquency. And the object of this book is to indicate some of the ways in which this knowledge of the causes of a man's delinquent conduct can be obtained. Only when we know the causes can we hope to apply the correct mode of treatment. To take an example from psycho-analysis, it is only when the repressed complexes are brought to light that the energy attached to the repressed emotions can be sublimated into more useful directions.

We have to regard the question from two points of view. We must consider our duty to Society, and we must consider our duty to the individual offender. And yet the two aspects are really but one. Just as no civilization can be healthy which is based upon a slave class, so no community can be healthy if it contains any large " criminal " class.

When we regard the actions of any person, or group of persons, we do well to put to ourselves constantly the question put to the prophet Jonah, " doest thou well to be angry ? ". In no case is this more desirable than in our dealings with offenders. Any attitude towards offenders may be pardoned, save one, that of anger. And it is our duty to consider whether there are not conditions in our present social arrangements which directly promote delinquency.

When we bring a man before a Court, we should not be content with assigning some penalty for his offence. We should first consider why it is that the offender is in rebellion against Society. It is certainly possible, by means of severity, to suppress many of the outward manifestations of rebellion. But the experience of ages has proved that this course is futile. We may take an illustration from psycho-analysis. We may regard a delinquency as an offending complex unacceptable to

# CONCLUSIONS    161

the rest of the mind. We may repress it into the unconscious, may think that we have destroyed it. But we have not destroyed it. In the unconscious it still exists, acting with dynamic force, escaping into consciousness in disguised forms, paving the way for neuroses. We must treat such a complex in a wholly different manner. This does not mean that we are to allow anti-social persons free permission to express themselves just as they may please. This is as absurd as the ridiculous travesty of psycho-analysis which is sometimes put forward by opponents of that science, and which attributes to psycho-analysts the doctrine that a man's repressed complexes should be brought into consciousness, and then should be allowed free play. The real solution for Society, as for the individual, is to explore the unconscious, to bring up the repressed complexes, and to surround the nuclei of the complexes with fresh emotions, while sublimating the original emotions (see Chapter III). Many tendencies which might otherwise lead to anti-social actions can be turned into directions which are useful to society. This has been realized. There are many impulses which act upon boys in early adolescence, love of change, desire for adventure, liking for mystery, wishes for a " gang " to which loyalty can be shown, and the like. All these have been well understood as likely to tend to delinquency. And we have seen many an instance in which they have directly so tended. But these impulses can be diverted into useful channels. And this fact has been taken advantage of by the Boy Scouts and similar movements. The only fear is that these movements may have a tendency to become stereotyped, and, in their turn, to thwart and deform the nature subjected to them.

That a man has not normal inhibitory powers is no reason for allowing him to be uncontrolled : rather, it is a greater reason for controlling and caring for him.

## 162 THE PSYCHOLOGY OF THE CRIMINAL

For example, we have seen that many epileptics are, by reason of their disease, specially prone to fall into delinquency. This may be a sound reason for not " punishing " them, but it is also a reason for placing them under care and control.

Again, we must see where the ideals of our Society have gone astray. These ideals are not fixed and immutable. Much of our delinquency is due to the pressure of Society, and, for this, Society is the responsible agent. We must, as a Society, face our conflicts. The process will be unpleasant, just as is the process of psycho-analysis. It will involve renunciation, and this is never agreeable. But the end will be peace, instead of conflict.

Faulty reaction on the part of an individual to Society may mean that Society has handled him incorrectly. A man may offend, and this applies specially to young offenders, because he does not know how to employ his normal, legitimate impulses. A barrel of powder will explode if we throw a lighted match into it ; it is the normal response to an improper mode of approach.

And we must see that our treatment of the offender is as helpful as we can make it. Let us study him, putting aside all our preconceived ideas. Let us try to discover why it is that he has failed to comply with Society's laws, and whether we cannot do something to put him in the way of conforming more easily. We must find what a man is able to do best, and then take pains to ensure that he does his best at that " job ". Only when we realize that in this direction lies our only road to peace, shall we escape from many of our present troubles. Let us try to discover in what direction a man can best be trained (and psychology will help us here), and then train him in that direction. Proper psychical employment, i.e. employment which will engage their best attention and endeavours, should be provided for all delinquents.

# CONCLUSIONS 163

In discovering an offender's complexes, grudges, and difficulties, we shall do much to discover our own as well. No man can attempt to conduct an analysis upon another without, in the process, learning much about himself. No society can study the offenders in its midst without a realization of its own shortcomings, which is humbling but hopeful. Hopeful, because in this way alone can it learn to remedy these shortcomings. And so the study of the offender leads not to despair, but to an enlightened optimism.

We have seen that the majority of our offenders commence their appearances in Court when quite young. As a consequence, it is essential to study them at that time. But their first appearance in Court is, usually, not the result of new and unprecedented conduct on their part. So we must go further in our study. Is our educational system all that we can desire in this respect ? The essential object of education is not the imparting of a certain amount of information. This has its value ; although there is reason to doubt whether the information so laboriously imparted is of much service to the recipients in their after-life. Still less is it the task of education to provide workers for our industrial system. The true aim of education is to place the child in such an attitude that his mind will be in harmony with the social body in which he will have to live, and that he may be a constructive factor in community life. Civilization implies socialization. And the real aim of education is to be a socializing force. It must attempt to ensure a healthy balance being formed by the moulding effect of the conflict between the herd instinct and the other primitive instincts (a conflict which is present in every individual), having due regard to the fact that only a certain amount of the psychic energy attached to the primitive instincts can be usefully or safely sublimated. As Tansley[1] says : " Attempt to divert

[1] " The New Psychology."

## 164 THE PSYCHOLOGY OF THE CRIMINAL

the whole available energy from primitive outlets leads, at the best, to a one-sided development of mind and character, for the primitive instincts, though they may be starved, cannot be destroyed. A certain amount of their energy can be sublimated with safety and advantage, but the effort cannot be unwisely pressed. The function of education should be to see that the complexes formed are such as to secure a fairly balanced allocation of the psychic energy available." That there must be adjustment to individual types does not mean that the child is to be placed at the mercy of any passing impulse, or that we must simply yield in the direction of least resistance. We must, however, remember that normal instincts always tend to vigorous action.

So much for education. Now, what of certain other obligations of Society ? The real assets of any community consist of the individuals who compose that community, and especially of the children. Under modern conditions the enormous majority of our children are subjected to the dangers, serious from a physical point of view, far more serious from a psychical point of view, of the streets. (Incidentally, we may, perhaps, wonder at the small percentage which falls into delinquency.) Juvenile delinquency often begins with the attempt to play in the streets contrary to town regulations. This play may be a nuisance to the community, but it is nothing less than the very life of the child. It is not merely desirable, it is an absolute obligation on the community, to see that every child has the opportunity of developing amid surroundings which are as perfect as they can be made. This is part of what may be termed the parental obligation of the community. The parental obligation has far too often been adopted only when a boy or girl has broken the law. It should have been adopted sooner. We may have to pass sentence, but we should also try to eliminate from our community life those elements which tend to cause

# CONCLUSIONS 165

delinquency in the normal boy. Poverty, overwork, and lack of opportunity for normal modes of expression, are all potent factors in the production of juvenile delinquency. Enforced unemployment may also act in this direction. Unsocial instincts are sometimes the result of lack of opportunity for social service.

The description which we have given of the methods of examination of the offenders will have indicated that this examination is an highly specialized matter, and that it takes much time. The ideal plan would be to examine every offender before he was dealt with by a Court. It is, really, as unreasonable to deal with an offender without due examination, as it is to prescribe for a patient without examination. We have pointed out that the particular act with which a man may happen to be charged is but a symptom, and may be quite an unimportant symptom. It may be said that many of the cases dealt with by Courts of Summary Jurisdiction are of a " trivial " nature, and are suitably dealt with by small fines. It is for others to decide upon what theory of punishment such fines are awarded. But we ought not even to contemplate the serious step of sentencing an offender to imprisonment without the most thorough examination. It is doubtful whether we ought even to place an offender on Probation without such examination. But such an extensive scheme as this is, at present, Utopian. Public opinion is not yet ready for it, and, further, we have not the necessary staff. Nor could we get the latter, even were the community willing to pay for them. At present the workers do not exist. We have to educate public opinion, and to train our workers. But we can, at least, make a beginning. And it would seem that our efforts should concentrate on the following classes.

1. *Young Offenders*. These are by far the most hopeful class. We have indicated the reasons for this. Their minds are more plastic. We have not to delve

# 166 THE PSYCHOLOGY OF THE CRIMINAL

so far for the causes of their delinquency. An anti-social feeling has not yet developed. Delinquent habits have not been formed. The effect of evil habit formation is of great importance in the production of delinquency. And the extent to which this habit formation has progressed must always be considered in giving a prognosis in any particular case. As Thorndyke[1] has said : " The likelihood that any mental state will occur in response to any situation is in proportion to the closeness of its inborn connexion therewith, to the frequency of the connexion therewith, and to the amount of satisfaction resulting." And so, in the treatment of offenders, one of the first requisites is to endeavour to induce such a fresh set of reactions on the part of the offender towards his environment that the resulting tendency will be away from delinquency. This must not, of course, lead us to overlook the necessity for modification of the environment, in cases where such modification may be possible.

The necessity for the special study of young offenders is, of course, recognized now. But much remains to be done.

2. *Repeated commission of the same kind of offence,* especially where the motive is not apparent, or where the almost definite certainty of detection should have been clear to the offender himself.

3. *Any other marked peculiarity about the offence.*[2]

The author holds strongly that competent medical and psychological selection of the cases for special examination should be instituted. He hopes to see the day when every Court will sit with an expert medical assessor. But, until that time comes, there should, at least, be careful selection of the cases for examination.

How, where, and by whom, is the examination to be conducted. It is clearly impossible, at present, to have

---

[1] " Elements of Psychology."
[2] See final paragraph on page 178.

## CONCLUSIONS 167

an expert attached to every Court, or even to every prison. And two plans seem feasible :

(a) To divide the country into convenient districts, each with a central prison, at which a specialist can be stationed, and at which there is a proper Hospital for the reception of cases remanded for examination. This we now have at Birmingham, and similar arrangements exist at some other large centres. Cases for examination should be sent to this prison, quite irrespective of the prison for ordinary cases arising in the particular part of the district in which the alleged offence has been committed. Objection will at once be taken on the grounds of expense. But let us consider. Any case which, although convicted, is kept out of prison represents a large direct saving, quite apart from indirect and future benefits. During a period of thirteen years the author dealt with more than 1,800 cases sent to him for examination from the City of Birmingham. Of these cases less than twenty-two per cent were ultimately sentenced to imprisonment. He does not suggest that the remaining seventy-eight per cent would have been so sentenced but for his report. But he claims, with some confidence, that a considerable proportion would have been so dealt with. Here is a large sum directly saved. And much increase is possible in this direction of economy, to take the argument on its very lowest grounds. And, while on this question of cost, it must be remembered that much expense is often incurred in preparing the case as regards the guilt or innocence of the prisoner before the case comes into Court ; yet this is only one element in the inquiry which should be made.

Objection is sometimes taken to sending such cases to prison for examination. The author thinks that this objection is not well founded. The patients should be treated under " hospital " conditions, the idea of " prison " should be kept out of sight. In Chapter II

## 168 THE PSYCHOLOGY OF THE CRIMINAL

we considered the various advantages which accrue from having the examination conducted in an institution. It would be possible to have Remand Homes for this purpose, apart from the prisons. But this would involve the building and staffing of new establishments. Whereas, in the prisons, we have buildings which could usually (as in Birmingham) be made suitable for the purpose, without undue alterations, and part of the staff is already in existence.

(*b*) To have a travelling mental expert in each district. This plan is now being tried in the State of Illinois. It might be combined with the first plan. It has certain advantages. On the other hand, the examiner would have to waste much time in travelling. And the examination might have to be made in unsuitable surroundings, and at a time when neither subject nor examiner was in the best mood. On the whole, the author thinks the first plan is preferable.

It is of the first importance that mental examination should be made before final trial and sentence. There is a movement in the United States for the legal trial to concern itself solely with the guilt or innocence of the offender with respect to the particular act with which he is charged, and that conviction should be followed by a mental and physical examination, upon the result of which examination the sentence should depend. The author deprecates this plan. Examinations made just after conviction are apt to be most misleading, as we pointed out in Chapter II. Examination before formal trial should be the rule. Some of the country Courts are very remiss in this way. We get convicted cases sent to us, with a note to the effect that mental examination appears to be desirable! Actual imbeciles are sometimes received in this way. There is no excuse for this practice in districts which possess a proper mental examiner. There should be no excuse in any district.

## CONCLUSIONS 169

With respect to the appointment of examiners, it is sometimes urged that these might be the officers of the district asylum. A knowledge of psychiatry is essential for the examiner, and he should be in close touch with the local psychiatrists. But there are special difficulties in dealing with offenders, and special problems in connexion with their cases, with which training in an asylum does not assist. The fact that a man has been for some years an officer in an asylum does not, in itself, qualify him for the investigation of offenders. Diplomas in psychological medicine are now being established by many of the medical examining bodies. To attain one of these should entail a knowledge of psychiatry, of mental defect, and of " criminology ". And, in course of time, the possession of such a diploma will be essential to the man or woman who desires to work in any one of these fields. Till that time comes, our chosen examiner must give proof of special study of, and experience with, offenders. And there is another point. If a subject has the idea that an attempt is being made to prove him insane or mentally defective, he will be likely to resent it, and very misleading results may be obtained from the examination. And it seems possible that the presence of an examiner who is known to be connected with the local asylum may easily produce this undesirable impression.

But we must train our examiners for the future. There is no school for this purpose in England, and there should be. In every university town there should be a centre of " criminological " research and teaching at which young medical graduates might learn their work. Of this work the mental examiner for the district should be the head, the director, and, above all, the inspirer. Formal lectures should be given to classes. Practical demonstrations would best be given informally and individually. There is an immense amount of valuable work waiting to be done in this

# 170 THE PSYCHOLOGY OF THE CRIMINAL

way. And such a scheme as is here outlined would give a great impetus to interest in this vital subject, as well as to the preparation of our future examiners.

We are sometimes asked, and we shall be more often asked in the future, what results we hope to get from the psycho-analysis of offenders. The answer will depend somewhat upon the environment of the subject. In addition to any conflict which may result from a repressed complex, there are often other " current " conflicts, which result from unfavourable surroundings at home, at work, or elsewhere. For a complete " cure " to ensue, these unfavourable conditions will have to be changed, and this is not always feasible. The case is other when the external conditions are more favourable, where the life would be peaceful save for the conflict in the unconscious. In such a subject, bringing to light the repressed complex may be all that is wanted. And such successes as the author has been able to record have been in such instances. So with the ordinary delinquent we must not expect miraculous results from unaided psycho-analysis. This is only to say that psycho-analysis does not claim to be a short and easy road to the final destruction of delinquency. But one thing we shall achieve, whatever the final result may be. We shall often be able to understand the cause of offences which would, otherwise, have been inexplicable. This is not only a great gain in itself. It is the necessary first step to any proper dealing with the offender.

It does not seem probable that psycho-analysis is likely to give us much help in many of the ordinary cases of burglary and larceny, at any rate for some time to come. Though even in some of these cases the author is hopeful that good results may come from psycho-analysis, if the case is taken in hand soon enough. Psycho-analysis holds out much more prospect in " sexual " offences, alcoholism, arson, and in cases

# CONCLUSIONS 171

of "kleptomania". We must, however, have two conditions : (1) Desire on the part of the subject for a cure, quite apart from his natural wish to escape from the legal consequences of some particular delinquency. (2) Sufficient time. It might be possible, in cases where psycho-analysis seems likely to be of service, to adjourn the case, say for six months, in order to see what psycho-analysis could achieve. There will be no undue rush on the part of offenders to avail themselves of this suggested arrangement. For many a day the ordinary offender will prefer to go through the routine of trial, imprisonment, and release. It would be of no use to try psycho-analysis with an unwilling subject. And sufficient time is usually of the essence of the problem. When it is remembered that the masters of psycho-analysis reckon that, for the average case, the treatment should extend over one year, it will be understood how important the time element is. It seems to the author that we shall have to deal with two classes of patients. One in whom a short analysis would be enough to clear up the difficulty. Such cases may be few in number, but they do exist. The other, larger class will always require prolonged analysis, which can never be shortened in any way.

But, while the author feels that the ideal plan is that of full examination before trial, yet he realizes that it may be many years before we reach our final goal in this respect. We shall continue to receive many prisoners whom we have had no opportunity of examining until after sentence. What can be done for these ? Examination of as many as is possible should be made. The necessary workers will be forthcoming when the value of the work is better understood. In some of these cases psycho-analysis will be found most useful. And by this and other means we shall be able to fortify our offender for the struggle which is sure to come on his release, by assisting him to form a plan for his better

## 172 THE PSYCHOLOGY OF THE CRIMINAL

adjustment to reality. And our responsibility to the offender surely should not cease when we open the gate for his discharge. After-care is an obligation on Society. And part of this after-care should consist of continued analysis in suitable cases. There is something to be said, also, for the indeterminate sentence, accompanied by a system of conditional release on " parole ", with due safeguards against the abuses to which this latter system is liable.

In dealing with our offenders we must not adopt the position that our " moral " standard is higher than theirs. We should only be entitled to do this if we accepted the conception of an " absolute " morality, and this conception we have seen reason to reject. Christianity has forbidden men to " judge ", deterministic science equally forbids them to " blame " their fellow men. We, who are not delinquents, have realized that a certain conformity with the arrangements of Society is necessary for the welfare of Society, and that it also tends, on balance, to our own happiness. Practically, we have made our adjustments to the demands of Society. And the best which we can do for the offender is to assist him to make these adjustments. But it is also our task to see that the demands of the Society are not unduly severe. The mediaeval lawmaker, strong in his supposed possession of a system of divinely given laws, was able to adopt the position that all men must conform to these laws or perish. It is impossible for us to adopt this position to-day, and, practically, no attempt to adopt it is made. Ultimately, our social arrangements must have the sanction that they tend, on balance, to the general welfare of Society. If they do not succeed in this, then they fail to attain their object.

It is common for discussions to take place as to the " reformatory " effect of prison or other institutional treatment. But even were all our institutions perfect,

## CONCLUSIONS 173

they could do no more than prepare an inmate for the real test, which comes when he leaves the institution. It is well to remember this, for often people talk as though some special form of institution was able to reform by itself, and quite apart from the co-operation of the subject. When our institutions are reproached with failure, we should remember that they are dealing with material not of their own choice, and with which other influences have already failed. Reformation is the result of a mental process within the man, and not of anything which he can obtain from without. We cannot do more than attempt to enable our patient to adapt himself to reality, to see where, and how, and why, his previous efforts have failed. We have to try and induce him to formulate a plan on which to base his future life. Absence of any plan of life is very characteristic of the delinquent class. We have to consider both the physical and mental sides of the patient. Too often have we contented ourselves with examination of the former, and have neglected the latter, because its examination was so much more difficult.

The important question is, How will our offender comport himself on his release from prison ? What will be his reaction to Society ? Have we done all we can to improve this attitude ? These questions are not new, they have exercised the minds of reformers for many years. Much has been done. Many old abuses have been remedied. Many of the evil conditions of former days have disappeared. Much of the dreariness of the prison atmosphere is a thing of the past. All this is to the good. But has not the real point been evaded ? Surely the solution of the questions asked above involves the recognition of something more than reforms of environment. There is something wanting in any scheme which assumes that all reform is contained in what is done to the prisoner, and which overlooks the importance of that creative impulse for regeneration

# 174 THE PSYCHOLOGY OF THE CRIMINAL

which must come from the man himself, and which comes, *inter alia*, through the exercise by the man of opportunities for self-expression and initiative, so far as these opportunities exist for him.

There is in every man something which is not affected by physical comforts, by financial encouragements, or by books. There is in every man a creative impulse, which can only be exercised by the man himself, along the paths of possible self-expression. We have to make opportunities for the man to express himself, to devise fresh methods to induce him to express himself, to arrange surroundings which will stimulate the desire for self-expression. Any proposed reform should be judged by this criterion, how far does it tend towards self-regeneration ? We are always inclined to overlook this, because to alter material conditions is so much easier a task.

The old retaliatory idea has been seen to be, not merely cruel, but devoid of useful results. In former days penal systems aimed at making prisoners amenable to rules until the end of their sentence, and, to some extent, they succeeded in this aim, although we are all too apt to confuse " discipline " with its expression. (Discipline is a far more elusive thing than gaining success in making men stand in straight lines and salute with precision). But to make offenders into good citizens on release, to arouse the creative impulse of which we have spoken, can it be said that we have succeeded in this ? As T. M. Osborne [1] has put it. The old system " endeavoured to make men industrious by driving them to work ; to make them virtuous by removing temptation ; to make them respect the law by forcing them to obey the orders of an autocrat ; to make them far-sighted by giving them no chance to exercise foresight ; to give them individual initiative by treating them in large groups ; in short, to prepare them again

[1] " Society and Prisons."

## CONCLUSIONS 175

for Society by placing them in conditions as unlike Society as they could be made." Surely the lives of inmates of any institution should be made as " normal " as is possible. Making unnecessary unhappiness and discomfort has never yet done good and never will. Every attempt must be made to induce the offender to realize that he is regarded as a patient who is being treated. If a penal system exists for the purpose of inducing men to live in a more social way on release, then they must have chances of so doing while under sentence.

The chief aim in all our examinations should be to obtain a clear definition of the individual offender, and of the factors which have operated to make him an offender. We have also to ascertain what desirable characteristics he may possess, cultivation of which would tend to make him a more valuable member of Society. It will, perhaps, be found that for a certain proportion of offenders the only solution is permanent segregation in a suitable institution. We must face this fact. To many the idea will be painful. It is one of the painful adjustments which Society has to make for its own health. It need hardly be said that the idea of " punishment " would not enter into any such scheme of permanent detention.

Our penal system should not be of a cast-iron character, which would only be suitable if men were machines. The offender has, hitherto, been regarded too much as a constant, whereas he is the most variable element in the problem. Above all else, we should have power and encouragement to try experiments.

The classification of prisoners to a far greater extent than is now done is one of the greatest desiderata. Every prisoner should be assigned to the prison which appears to be best suited to his case. Nothing should be allowed to stand in the way of this. There should, really, be no such thing as a legal sentence too short to " make it worth while " considering where and how the

## 176 THE PSYCHOLOGY OF THE CRIMINAL

case would best be treated. But even without legal abolition of short sentences, it would be possible, now, to have a central examining and classifying prison for prisoners with the longer sentences. This plan is being tried in the State of New York. A central prison has been established, to which all men with a sentence of one year or more are sent, and at which they receive a most thorough examination, before being drafted to what are considered the most suitable prisons for each particular kind of case.

There are certain cases for which Probation is not considered suitable, or for which it has been tried and found wanting. A Borstal sentence may for some reason, be impracticable, e.g. the offender may be over twenty-one years of age. Except for fines and short sentences of imprisonment the law seems, in such cases, to be bankrupt. If the offender happens to be a mental defective, something can be done. But it would seem unreasonable that the offender should be denied desirable help, because he is not mentally defective.

The author deprecates undue stress being laid upon calendar age in the grading of offenders. There are many lads of 18 who are not more developed, physically or mentally, than is the average boy of 14. And the converse of this statement is equally true. The fixation of an arbitrary age for the operation of the law affecting " children " would seem to be unfortunate.

And a few final words. In his analyses, the author feels that he may have laid himself open to the charge that he excuses crime. He desires to make his position clear. While he believes that scientific knowledge, not to speak of other reasons, forbids us to blame the offender, he has no wish to palliate or to condone the offender's anti-social actions. Our efforts should be turned in the direction of an attempt to investigate and so to explain the causes of anti-social conduct.

# CONCLUSIONS 177

The question really comes to this: What does our judicial and penal system accomplish for us? Does it really serve Society? Or may it not be that it is doing more harm than good? When we reflect upon these questions, have we more than ignorant guesses to offer by way of answers? Are not many of our views as to the sources of anti-social actions, and as to the motives which produce or inhibit those actions, nothing more than quite unjustified assumptions? Has not the day come for a re-examination of our penal system and of its bases, in the light of our newer and fuller scientific knowledge, and in the hope that we might devise something better?

We may draw an analogy from other branches of science. These only make progress in so far as they study causations. Is there any reason why the study of offenders should be an exception to this rule? Is it not true that in no other branch of science have we proceeded so ignorantly, and yet with so much confidence? We only made progress in our control of physical infectious diseases when we endeavoured to ascertain their character, their causes, and the conditions which govern their propagation. Have we made any serious attempt to gather any scientific knowledge of a similar kind for the better understanding of offences, and of the conditions of their propagation in the community, and so of their control?

We have lately passed through the greatest of international wars. And we are making some attempts to ascertain the causes which govern the outbreak and the spread of hostility between nations. And we have at last recognized that " war " can never " end war ". Again, we see that our old methods of industrial strife are abominably wasteful, and appear likely to end in the complete paralysis of productive industry. The more thoughtful of our rulers are seeing that mere palliatives are useless, are striving for some means of

# 178 THE PSYCHOLOGY OF THE CRIMINAL

terminating this conflict, and of avoiding the complete breakdown of modern civilization which appears only too likely to be the ultimate conclusion. But when we consider the undying civil war which delinquency is waging against Society, sapping the basis of our social order, what have we to offer as solutions ? Is it not true to say that here we have been, and still are, content with mere assumptions ? These assumptions have been concerned, some with the nature of the offender, some with the conditions which govern the propagation of delinquency, and some with the supposed effects of " punishment ". Many of these assumptions are legacies derived from our prehistoric ancestors, and some have been handed down to us from religious systems of the past.

The mass of human failures which now has to be re-pressed at the cost of enormous sums of money, and of much unprofitable labour, represents a dynamic force of vast magnitude. It must, if possible, be changed from a destructive to a constructive force. The problem is abstruse and complicated. But its true solution lies in an intensive and deliberate study of the offender, as an individual, in all his Protean aspects. And for this investigation we have the material ready to our hands at our Courts and in our prisons.

A very strong case exists for the routine investigation of all persons charged with " sex " offences. There is general agreement that the incidence of mental abnorm-ality in offenders of this class is very high. The author investigated 100 consecutive cases (50 of indecent assault and 50 of indecent exposure). In only 17 of these no mental abnormality was found. The remaining 83 were insane, mentally defective, epileptic, or the subjects of marked mental conflict.[1]

[1] " Lancet," 1924, Vol. I, pp. 643 ff.

# APPENDIX

I. Interest in the question was re-awakened by the trial of Ronald True in 1922.[1] The then Lord Chancellor appointed a committee to consider what changes, if any, were desirable in the existing practice and procedure. This committee was presided over by Lord Justice Atkin (now Lord Atkin). The committee was entirely legal in its personnel, but it considered medical evidence. The said evidence was, however, of a conflicting character. The committee reported to the effect that the McNaughten rules should be maintained, but that an accused person should be held irresponsible for a criminal offence when the act was committed under an impulse which he was, by mental disease, in substance, deprived of any power to resist. No attempt has been made to alter the present practice in accordance with the committee's recommendation. Were the proposed new criterion to be adopted it would probably occasion disputes quite as frequent and as acrimonious as those which occur under the existing rules. It is impossible to say, in any particular case, that an impulse was irresistible ; all that can be said is that the impulse did not appear to have been successfully resisted. If anyone will attempt to put into accurate language the statement about a man that *he* could not control *his* actions, not merely the difficulty but the impossibility of the task will soon be perceived. So we remain, for the time being, with the McNaughten rules. In actual practice much depends upon the precise manner in which the pertinent questions are put to the medical witnesses and upon the manner in which the presiding judge charges the jury. There has, however, been one recent improvement. The Infanticide Act, 1922, renders it unnecessary to put a woman on her trial for the murder of her newly-born child ; she can now be charged with the lesser offence of infanticide. Formerly it was necessary to sentence to death a woman found guilty of such an offence. It was fully understood that the death penalty would not be exacted. But to avoid the painful formality of solemnly pronouncing a sentence of death the McNaughten rules were often strained to their utmost limit of elasticity.

[1] Vide " Journal of Mental Science," 1922 ; " The Case of Ronald True," by M. Hamblin Smith ; also " Trial of Ronald True," by D. Carswell (William Hodge & Co., 1925).

# 180 THE PSYCHOLOGY OF THE CRIMINAL

II. The doubt expressed by the author in the original edition of this book has been accentuated by experience. It has been almost impossible to ascertain the real facts ; for enthusiasm, on either side of the controversy, largely vitiated the value of statistics. But the profits accruing from the sale of illicit alcohol were very large. And there appears to be but little doubt that conflicts between the police and dealers in illicit alcohol, and between rival gangs of such dealers, gravely increased the incidence of serious crime. It is certain that there was much corruption. And there was yet another, and a still more serious result. It was well-known that this particular law was contemptuously ignored and largely evaded ; and this occasioned a wide-spread detraction from the respect felt for law in general. No worse ailment can occur in any community. Recent events indicate that the repeal of " prohibition " is only a matter of time. The whole experience has been unfortunate. Prior to the enactment of " prohibition ", there was arising, in influential American circles, a strong feeling against the excessive use of alcohol ; and this could not have failed, in time, to produce its effect. Enthusiasts for legal action, in this as in other directions, seem unable to remember the old warning : " He that believeth shall not make haste".

III. 16. *Koh's Coloured Blocks.* This test consists in the reproduction, by means of coloured wooden blocks, of a series of patterns of gradually-increasing difficulty presented to the subject. The earlier patterns in the series are very simple, the later patterns are of decidedly greater difficulty. The point at which the subject fails is noted.

17. *The " Passalong " Test.* This was invented by Mr. W. P. Alexander, of Glasgow University.[1] The test consists in the manipulation of coloured blocks placed in a frame, so as to produce a pattern shown on a card. There is a graduated series of these patterns ; the first should be reproduced by the average five-year-old child, the final pattern requires quite a high grade of intelligence.

[1] "British Journal of Psychology," Vol. xxiii, 1932.

# INDEX

## A

*ADLER*, 90
Adolescence, 150, 161.
Alcohol, 14, 25, 110, 117, 122
136, 139, 155, 180.
Alternating personality, 72.
American army, Mental tests
in, 49, 52, 136.
Amnesia, 73, 113.
Anatomical theory of criminality, 22.
Anti-social feeling, 29, 118.
Anxiety neurosis, 107.
Aussage test, 38.

## B

BALL in field test, 40.
*Binet*, 33, 134.
Birmingham, 167.
Borstal system, 117, 151, 176.
*Burt*, 51.

## C

CANCELLATION test, 41.
Censorship, 74.
Childhood, 122, 128, 129.
Classification of offenders, 175.
Cocainism, 157.
Code test, 50.
Complex, 68, 89.
Compulsion neurosis, 107, 109.
Conduct the result of mental
life, 8, 21, 23, 24.

Conflict, Mental, 25, 28, 69, 97,
115, 170.
——, Examples of 82, 84, 100,
119.
Constellation, 69.
Constitutional inferiors, 150.
Court, True function of, 16,
160, 165.
Crime, Definition of, 2.
Criminal type, 2, 15, 22.
Criminalism, 149.
Criminality, Theories of, 13.

## D

DEFECT, Mental, 133, 137.
——, Causes of, 139.
——, Definitions of, 135, 136.
——, Delinquency and, 138.
Degeneration, Stigmata of, 22,
30.
Delinquency, Juvenile, 164.
Determinism, 5, 9, 76, 91, 103.
Deterrent punishment, 5.
*Devon*, 159.
Dipsomania, 110, 170.
Dreams, Condensation in, 85.
——, Content of, 86.
——, Displacement in, 86.
——, Dramatization in, 87.
——, Interpretation of, 85, 87,
91.
——, Symbolization in, 86.

## E

EDUCATION, 111, 129, 163.
Educational tests, 35.

181

# 182  THE PSYCHOLOGY OF THE CRIMINAL

*Ellis, Havelock*, 123.
Emotional control, 62.
Emotional instability, 148.
Epilepsy, 29, 114, 143, 162.
Epileptic automatism, 144.
—— equivalents, 144.
Ethical discrimination test, 50.
—— perception test, 50.

### F

FEEBLE-MINDED, 134.
Fixation, 121, 156.
Foreconscious, 68.
Form boards, 37.
Free association, 83.
Free will, 1, 9, 61.
*Freud*, 65, 69, 77, 85, 95, 101, 111, 113, 121.
Fugue states, 72.

### G

GLANDS, Ductless, 30.
*Goring*, 17, 31.
*Groszman*, 21.
Group tests, 51.

### H

HABIT formation, 29, 117.
*Halsbury*, 2.
*Hamon*, 2.
*Haggarty*, 56.
*Hart*, 69.
*Healy*, 34, 42, 99, 128, 140.
Heilbronner's test, 41.
Heredity, 14, 25, 128, 131.
Homicidal impulses, 110.
*Howard*, 7.
Hypnotism, 79.
Hysteria, 107, 115.

### I

IDIOTS, 135.
Inferiors, Constitutional, 150.
Information, Tests for, 43.
Imbeciles, 135.
Impulse, Irresistible, 109, 110.
Insanity, 31, 75, 114, 120, 133, 137.
Instincts, Primitive, 66, 96.

### J

*JONES, Ernest*, 77, 125.
*Jung*, 91.
Juvenile delinquency, 164.

### K

KLEPTOMANIA, 109, 171.
Koh's test, 180.
*Kraft Ebing*, 123.

### L

*LACASSAGNE*, 159.
*Lombroso*, 21, 25, 30, 96.
*Low, Barbara*, 88.
Lying, Pathological, 149.

### M

*McCONNELL*, 76.
*McDougall*, 66, 102.
McNaughten judgment, 10.
*Marro*, 151.
Masturbation, 124.
*Mercier*, 7, 154.
Memory, Loss of. *See* "Amnesia."
Mental age, 47, 135, 137.

# INDEX

183

Mental conflict. *See* "Conflict."

Mental defect. *See* "Defect."

Mental tests, 32, 180.

——, Difficulties in, 55, 58.

——, Interpretation of, 32, 46, 56.

Morality, 3, 172.

Moral imbecility, 147, 152.

Moral sense, 153.

Morons, 135.

Morphinism, 157.

### N

NEURASTHENIA, 106.

Neurosis, 73, 106, 111.

Nomadism, 149.

### O

*OSBORNE*, 174.

*Otis*, 52, 54.

### P

PARANOIA, 120, 148.

Paranoid personality, 148.

Passalong test, 180.

Personality, Alternating, 72

——, Inadequate, 147.

——, Paranoid, 148.

Physical defects as causes of mental conflict, 28.

—— —— as influences to delinquency, 27

Pictorial completion test, 42.

Pictures, Interpretation of, 39.

Pleasure principle, 77.

Poverty, 14.

Preconscious, 68.

Probation system, 17, 152, 158, 165, 176.

Psycho-analysis, 24, 71, 78, 90, 97, 129, 157, 170.

——, Difficulties in, 71, 90, 92, 105, 171.

—— in Court work, 84, 93, 115, 129, 132, 170.

——, Objections to, 101.

——, Transference in, 89.

Psychological view of crime, 23.

Psycho-neuroses, 73.

Psychopaths, 146.

Psychopathy, Sexual, 123, 149.

Puberty, 150.

Punishment, Deterrent, 5.

——, Reformatory, 6, 172.

——, Retaliatory, 4, 174.

### R

REALITY principle, 77.

Recidivism, 17.

Reformatory punishment, 6, 172.

Regression, 125.

Repression, 71.

Responsibility, 8, 77, 179.

Retaliatory punishment, 4, 174.

*Rosanoff*, 10, 77, 108, 147.

### S

SELF expression, 174.

Senility, 125, 136.

Sex instinct, 67, 98, 101 121.

Sexual offences, 99, 113, 170, 178.

—— psychopathy, 123, 149.

Social disability, 116.

Special abilities and disabilities, 141.

Speech, Impediments in, 29.

*Spinoza*, 62, 103, 125.

*Stephen*, 9, 11, 62, 154.

*Stoddart*, 146.

Stigmata. *See* " Degeneration."

# 184 THE PSYCHOLOGY OF THE CRIMINAL

Sublimation, 71.
Subnormal offenders, 142.
Substitution, 112.
Substitution delinquences, 99.
Suggestibility, 39, 40, 42, 127.
Suggestion, 61, 104.
Symbolization, 74.

### T

*TANSLEY*, 163.
Tests. *See* " Mental tests."
*Terman*, 33, 40, 138.
*Thorndyke*, 166.
Tobacco, 157.
Transference in psycho-analysis, 89.
*Tredgold*, 140, 141.

### U

UNCONSCIOUS mind, 64.

### V

VERBALIST type, 35, 138, 140.

### W

WILL power, 61.
Word association, 80.

### Y

YOUNG offenders, 17, 105, 163.

*Printed by Jarrold & Sons Ltd. Norwich*